FLASH IN
THE PAN

FLASH IN THE PAN

COLLINS & BROWN

The Good Housekeeping website is
www.goodhousekeeping.co.uk

ISBN 978-1-909397-02-6

A catalogue record for this book is available from
the British Library.

Reproduction by Dot Gradations Ltd, UK
Printed and bound by
1010 Printing International Ltd, China

This book can be ordered direct from the publisher.
Contact the marketing department, but try your
bookshop first.

www.anovabooks.com

NOTES

Both metric and imperial measures are given for
the recipes. Follow either set of measures, not a
mixture of both, as they are not interchangeable.

All spoon measures are level.
1 tsp = 5ml spoon; 1 tbsp = 15ml spoon.

Ovens and grills must be preheated to the specified
temperature.

Medium eggs should be used except where
otherwise specified. Free-range eggs are
recommended.

Note that some recipes contain raw or lightly
cooked eggs. The young, elderly, pregnant women
and anyone with an immune-deficiency disease
should avoid these because of the slight risk
of salmonella.

Contents

Sides and Salads

Stir-frying Vegetables

Stir-frying is perfect for non-starchy vegetables, as the quick cooking preserves their colour, freshness and texture.

Perfect stir-frying

- Cut everything into small pieces of uniform size so that they cook quickly and evenly.
- If you're cooking onions or garlic with the vegetables, don't keep them in the high heat for too long or they will burn.
- Add liquids towards the end of cooking so they don't evaporate.

You will need 450g (1lb) vegetables, 1–2 tbsp vegetable oil, 2 crushed garlic cloves, 2 tbsp soy sauce, 2 tsp sesame oil.

1 Cut the vegetables into even-size pieces. Heat the oil in a large wok or frying pan until smoking-hot. Add the garlic and cook for a few seconds, then remove and put to one side.

2 Add the vegetables to the wok, then toss and stir them. Keep them moving constantly as they cook, which will take 4–5 minutes.

3 When the vegetables are just tender, but still with a slight bite, turn off the heat. Put the garlic back into the wok and stir well. Add the soy sauce and sesame oil, toss and serve.

Stir-fried Beans with Cherry Tomatoes

Hands-on time: 10 minutes
Cooking time: about 8 minutes

350g (12oz) green beans, trimmed
2 tsp olive oil
1 large garlic clove, crushed
150g (5oz) cherry or baby plum
  tomatoes, halved
2 tbsp freshly chopped
  flat-leafed parsley
salt and freshly ground black pepper

1 Cook the green beans in boiling salted water for 4–5 minutes, then drain well.

2 Heat the oil in a wok or large frying pan over a high heat. Stir-fry the beans with the garlic and tomatoes for 2–3 minutes until the beans are tender and the tomatoes are just beginning to soften without losing their shape. Season well with salt and ground black pepper, stir in the parsley and serve.

Serves 6

Mushrooms with Cashew Nuts

Hands-on time: 5 minutes
Cooking time: about 8 minutes

1 tbsp vegetable oil

25g (1oz) unsalted cashew nuts

225g (8oz) brown-cap mushrooms, sliced

1 tbsp lemon juice

4 tbsp freshly chopped coriander, plus sprigs to garnish

1 tbsp single cream (optional)

salt and freshly ground black pepper

1 Heat the oil in a wok or large frying pan. Add the cashew nuts and cook over a high heat for 2–3 minutes until golden. Add the mushrooms and cook for a further 2–3 minutes until tender, stirring frequently.

2 Stir in the lemon juice and coriander and season to taste with salt and ground black pepper. Heat until bubbling. Remove the pan from the heat and stir in the cream if you like. Adjust the seasoning if necessary, and serve immediately, garnished with coriander sprigs.

SAVE EFFORT

For a simple alternative dish try **Chinese Garlic Mushrooms**: replace the nuts with 2 garlic cloves, crushed, and stir-fry for only 20 seconds before adding the mushrooms. Replace the lemon juice with rice wine or dry sherry.

Serves 4

Veggie Spring Rolls

Hands-on time: about 20 minutes
Cooking time: about 30 minutes

150g (5oz) cooked rice vermicelli
150g (5oz) bamboo shoots
1 carrot, coarsely grated
3 spring onions, finely sliced
1 garlic clove, crushed
2ml (1fl oz) soy sauce
1 tbsp oil, plus extra to brush
large handful fresh coriander, finely
  chopped
1-2 tsp toasted sesame oil
6 x 20.5cm (8in) square spring roll
  wrappers

1 Preheat oven to 200°C (180°C fan)
mark 6. Roughly chop vermicelli
into bite-sized pieces; put into a large
bowl. Roughly cut bamboo shoots into
matchsticks and add to vermicelli
with the carrot, spring onions, garlic,
soy sauce and some seasoning.

2 Heat the oil in a large wok or frying
pan over high heat and add vermicelli
mixture. Cook for a few min, stirring
occasionally, until the veg are tender.
Take off heat and leave to cool.

3 Mix in coriander and sesame oil; check
seasoning. Put a spring roll wrapper on
a board and spoon ⅙ of the vermicelli
mixture along one edge, leaving a
2.5cm (1in) border on each side. Fold
in the sides over the filling, then roll
up (encasing the filling), sealing with
a little water. Repeat with remaining
mixture and wrappers.

4 Arrange the spring rolls seam-side
down on a non-stick baking tray and
brush with oil. Cook in the oven for
20-25min until golden brown. Allow
to cool for a few min, then serve with
sweet chilli sauce.

Makes 6 large
Spring Rolls

The Asian Storecupboard

Rice and noodles are the staple foods. The following items, used in many Asian dishes, are available in most large supermarkets and Asian food shops.

Spices

- **Chinese five-spice powder** is made from star anise, fennel seeds, cinnamon, cloves and Sichuan pepper. It has a strong liquorice-like flavour and should be used sparingly.

- **Kaffir lime leaves**, used in South-east Asian cooking for their lime-lemon flavour, are glossy leaves used whole but not eaten – rather like bay leaves. Use grated lime zest as a substitute.

- **Tamarind paste** has a delicately sour flavour; use lemon juice as a substitute.

Sauces

- **Soy sauce** – made from fermented soya beans and, usually, wheat – is the most common flavouring in Chinese and South-east Asian cooking. There are light and dark soy sauces; the dark kind is slightly sweeter and tends to darken the food. It will keep indefinitely.
- **Thai fish sauce** is a salty condiment with a distinctive, pungent aroma. It is used in many South-east Asian dishes. You can buy it in most large supermarkets and Asian food stores. It will keep indefinitely.
- **Thai green curry paste** is a blend of spices such as green chillies, coriander and lemongrass. Thai red curry paste contains fresh and dried red chillies and ginger. Once opened, store in a sealed container in the fridge for up to one month.
- **Chilli sauce** is made from fresh red chillies, vinegar, salt and sugar; some versions include other ingredients such as garlic or ginger. Sweet chilli sauce is a useful standby for adding piquancy to all kinds of dishes.
- **Black bean sauce** is made from fermented black beans, salt and ginger. Salty and pungent on its own, it adds richness to many stir-fry dishes.
- **Yellow bean sauce** is a thick, salty, aromatic yellow-brown purée of fermented yellow soy beans, flour and salt.
- **Hoisin sauce**, sometimes called barbecue sauce, is a thick, sweet-spicy red-brown sauce made from mashed soya beans, garlic, chillies and other spices.
- **Oyster sauce** is a smooth brown sauce made from oyster extract, wheat flour and other flavourings. It doesn't taste fishy, but adds a 'meaty' flavour to stir-fries and braises.
- **Plum sauce**, made from plums, ginger, chillies, vinegar and sugar, is traditionally served with duck or as a dip.

Coconut milk

- **Canned coconut milk** is widely available, but if you can't find it, use blocks of creamed coconut or coconut powder, following the pack instructions to make the amount of liquid you need.

Canned vegetables

- **Bamboo shoots**, available sliced or in chunks, they have a mild flavour; rinse before use.
- **Water chestnuts** have a very mild flavour but add a lovely crunch to stir-fried and braised dishes.

Other ingredients

- **Dried mushrooms** feature in some Chinese recipes; they need to be soaked in hot water for 30 minutes before use.
- **Dried shrimps and dried shrimp paste (blachan)** are often used in South-east Asian cooking. The pungent smell becomes milder during cooking and marries with the other ingredients. These are often included in ready-made sauces and spice pastes, and are not suitable for vegetarians.
- **Mirin** is a sweet rice wine from Japan; if you can't find it, use dry or medium sherry instead
- **Rice wine** is often used in Chinese cooking; if you can't find it, use dry sherry instead.
- **Rice vinegar** is clear and milder than other vinegars. Use white wine vinegar or cider vinegar as a substitute.

Which oil to use?

- **Groundnut (peanut)** oil has a mild flavour and is widely used in China and South-east Asia. It is well suited to stir-frying and deep-frying as it has a high smoke point and can therefore be used at high temperatures.
- **Vegetable oil** may be pure rapeseed oil, or a blend of corn, soya bean, rapeseed or other oils. It usually has a bland flavour and is suitable for stir-frying.
- **Sesame oil** has a distinctive nutty flavour; it is best used in marinades or added as a seasoning to stir-fried dishes just before serving.

Sesame and Cabbage Rolls

Hands-on time: 30 minutes, plus soaking
Cooking time: about 15 minutes, plus cooling

50g (2oz) dried shiitake mushrooms

3 tbsp sesame oil

4 garlic cloves, crushed

4 tbsp sesame seeds

450g (1lb) cabbage, finely shredded

1 bunch of spring onions, trimmed
   and chopped

225g can bamboo shoots, drained

3 tbsp soy sauce

½ tsp caster sugar

2 × 270g packs filo pastry

1 large egg, beaten

vegetable oil to deep-fry

Spiced Plum Sauce or Thai Chilli
   Dipping Sauce to serve

1 Put the mushrooms in a heatproof
   bowl and cover with boiling water.
   Soak for 20 minutes.

2 Heat the sesame oil in a wok or
   large frying pan. Add the garlic and
   sesame seeds and fry gently until
   golden brown. Add the cabbage and
   spring onions and fry, stirring, for
   3 minutes.

3 Drain and slice the mushrooms. Add
   them to the pan with the bamboo
   shoots, soy sauce and sugar and stir
   until well mixed. Remove the pan
   from the heat and leave to cool.

4 Cut the filo pastry into 24 × 18cm
   (7in) squares. Keep the filo squares
   covered with a damp teatowel as you
   work. Place one square of filo pastry
   on the worksurface and cover with
   a second square. Place a heaped
   tablespoon of the cabbage mixture
   across the centre of the top square to
   within 2.5cm (1in) of the ends. Fold
   the 2.5cm (1in) ends of pastry over
   the filling. Brush one unfolded edge
   of the pastry with a little beaten egg,
   then roll up to make a thick parcel
   shape. Shape the remaining pastry
   and filling in the same way to make
   12 parcels.

5 Heat a 5cm (2in) depth of oil in a
   deep-fryer or large heavy-based
   saucepan to 180°C (test by frying
   a small cube of bread; it should

Makes 12

brown in 40 seconds). Fry the rolls in batches for about 3 minutes or until crisp and golden. Remove with a slotted spoon and drain on kitchen paper; keep them warm while you fry the remainder. Serve hot with a sauce for dipping.

Perfect Deep-frying

Shellfish and small pieces of fish, carrots, broccoli, onions, courgettes, aubergines, mushrooms, peppers and cauliflower are all good deep-fried in a light batter.

To serve four, you will need:
About 900g (2lb) mixed vegetables (such as aubergines, broccoli, cauliflower, red peppers), cut into small, similar-size pieces, vegetable oil to deep-fry, 125g (4oz) plain flour, plus extra to coat, 125g (4oz) cornflour, a pinch of salt, 1 medium egg yolk, 300ml (½ pint) sparkling water.

1 Prepare the vegetables and cut into small pieces (no more than 2cm (¾in) thick). Dry well on kitchen paper.
2 Heat the oil in a deep-fryer to 170°C (a small cube of bread should brown in 40 seconds).

3   To make the batter, lightly whisk together the flour, cornflour, salt, egg yolk and water.

4   Coat the vegetables lightly with flour, then dip into the batter.

5   Fry in batches, a few pieces at a time, until the batter is crisp and golden brown. Don't put too many vegetables in the pan at once (if you do, the temperature drops and the vegetables take longer to cook and become greasy). Remove with a slotted spoon and drain on kitchen paper before serving.

Vegetable Tempura

🍴 **Hands-on time:** 20 minutes
Cooking time: 15 minutes

125g (4oz) plain flour, plus 2 tbsp extra
to sprinkle

2 tbsp cornflour

2 tbsp arrowroot

125g (4oz) cauliflower, cut into
small florets

2 large carrots, cut into matchsticks

16 button mushrooms

2 courgettes, sliced

2 red peppers, seeded and sliced

vegetable oil to deep-fry

salt and freshly ground black pepper

fresh coriander sprigs to garnish

For the dipping sauce:

25g (1oz) fresh root ginger, peeled
and grated

4 tbsp dry sherry

3 tbsp soy sauce

1 Sift the flour, cornflour and
arrowroot into a large bowl with a
pinch each of salt and ground black
pepper. Gradually whisk in 300ml
(½ pint) ice-cold water to form a thin
batter. Cover the bowl and chill
in the fridge.

2 To make the dipping sauce, put
the ginger, sherry and soy sauce
in a heatproof bowl and pour over
200ml (7fl oz) boiling water. Stir
well to mix, then put to one side.

3 Put the vegetables in a large bowl
and sprinkle over 2 tbsp flour. Toss
well to coat. Heat the oil in a wok or
deep-fryer to 170°C (test by frying a
small cube of bread; it should brown
in 40 seconds).

4 Dip a handful of the vegetables
into the batter, then remove with
a slotted spoon, taking up a lot of
the batter with the vegetables. Add
to the hot oil and deep-fry for 3–5
minutes until crisp and golden.
Remove with a slotted spoon and
drain on kitchen paper; keep them
hot while you cook the remaining
batches. Serve immediately,
garnished with coriander sprigs and
accompanied by the dipping sauce.

Serves 4

Thai Noodle Salad

Hands-on time: 20 minutes, plus soaking
Cooking time: about 8 minutes

200g (7oz) sugarsnap peas, trimmed
250g pack Thai stir-fry rice noodles
100g (3½oz) cashew nuts
300g (11oz) carrots, cut into batons
10 spring onions, sliced on
  the diagonal
300g (11oz) bean sprouts
20g (¾oz) fresh coriander, roughly
  chopped, plus sprigs to garnish
1 red bird's eye chilli, seeded and
  finely chopped (see Safety Tip,
  page 28)
2 tsp sweet chilli sauce
4 tbsp sesame oil
6 tbsp soy sauce
juice of 2 limes
salt and freshly ground black pepper

HEALTHY TIP

Red bird's eye chillies are always
very hot. The smaller they are, the
hotter they are.

1 Bring a pan of salted water to the boil and blanch the sugarsnap peas for 2–3 minutes until just tender to the bite. Drain and refresh under cold water.

2 Put the noodles into a bowl, cover with boiling water and leave to soak for 4 minutes. Rinse under cold water and drain very well.

3 Toast the cashews in a dry frying pan until golden – about 5 minutes.

4 Put the sugarsnaps in a large glass serving bowl. Add the carrots, spring onions, bean sprouts, chopped coriander, chopped chilli, cashews and noodles. Mix together the chilli sauce, oil, soy sauce and lime juice and season well with salt and ground black pepper. Pour over the salad, toss together, garnish with coriander sprigs and serve.

Serves 4

Prawn Noodle Salad

🍴 **Hands-on time:** 15 minutes

300g bag cooked rice noodles
juice of 2 limes
1 tbsp fish sauce
2 tsp light soft brown sugar
1 red chilli, seeded and finely chopped
    (see Safety Tip)
2.5cm (1in) piece fresh root ginger,
    peeled and grated
2 carrots, peeled into ribbons
300g (11oz) bean sprouts
200g (7oz) sugarsnap peas, sliced
350g (12oz) cooked king prawns,
    peeled and deveined
a large handful of fresh mint
    leaves, chopped
40g (1½oz) roasted salted peanuts,
    roughly chopped

1 Put the rice noodles into a heatproof bowl and pour boiling water from the kettle over them until they are covered. Cover with cling film. Put to one side for 5 minutes to heat through. Drain well and put the noodles back into the bowl.

2 In a separate bowl, stir together the lime juice, fish sauce, sugar, chilli and ginger. Add the vegetables, prawns and mint to the drained noodles, then pour the dressing on and toss through. Garnish with peanuts and serve.

SAFETY TIP
Chillies can be quite mild to blisteringly hot, depending on the type of chilli and its ripeness. Taste a small piece first to check it's not too hot for you. Be extremely careful when handling chillies not to touch or rub your eyes with your fingers, or they will sting. Wash knives immediately after handling chillies. As a precaution, use rubber gloves when preparing them, if you like.

Serves 4

Chilli Beef Noodle Salad

🍴 **Hands-on time:** 15 minutes, plus soaking

150g (5oz) dried rice noodles
50g (2oz) rocket leaves
125g (4oz) sliced cold roast beef
125g (4oz) sunblush tomatoes,
    chopped

For the Thai dressing:

juice of 1 lime
1 lemongrass stalk, outside leaves
    discarded, finely chopped
1 red chilli, seeded and chopped (see
    Safety Tip, page 28)
2 tsp finely chopped fresh root ginger
2 garlic cloves, crushed
1 tbsp Thai fish sauce
3 tbsp extra virgin olive oil
salt and freshly ground black pepper

1 Put the noodles in a large bowl and
  pour boiling water over them to
  cover. Put to one side for 15 minutes.
2 To make the dressing, whisk
  together the lime juice, lemongrass,
  chilli, ginger, garlic, fish sauce and
  oil in a small bowl and season with
  salt and ground black pepper.
3 While they are still warm, drain the
  noodles well, put in a large bowl and
  toss with the dressing. Leave to cool.
4 Just before serving, toss the rocket
  leaves, sliced beef and tomatoes
  through the noodles.

SAVE EFFORT

For an easy alternative, use roast
pork instead of beef.

Serves 4

Soups
and Curries

Chicken Noodle Soup

🍴 **Hands-on time:** 15 minutes
Cooking time: 23 minutes

2 medium eggs
1.6 litres (2¾ pints) chicken stock
1 tbsp light soy sauce
2cm (¾in) piece fresh root ginger,
    thickly sliced
1 garlic clove, bruised
3 skinless chicken breasts
2 carrots, finely chopped
125g (4oz) fine or medium noodles
150g (5oz) oyster mushrooms
salt and freshly ground black pepper
4 spring onions, finely sliced,
    to garnish

1 Bring a small pan of water to the boil; simmer the eggs for 7 minutes. Drain, put in a bowl and cover with cold water.

2 Meanwhile, heat the chicken stock, soy sauce, ginger and garlic in a large pan and bring to the boil. Add the chicken, reduce the heat and simmer for 12 minutes until the meat is cooked through. Lift the meat out of the broth and on to a board. Discard the ginger and garlic. Add the carrots and noodles to the broth. Simmer for 4 minutes and season to taste. Meanwhile, slice the chicken breast and shell and halve the eggs.

3 Divide the soup among four bowls (adding a little more boiling water if needed), top each with a quarter of the chicken slices, a quarter of the mushrooms and half an egg. Scatter over the spring onions and serve.

SAVE EFFORT

This Japanese-style soup is full of light flavours – add a chopped red chilli if you like for an easy way to spice it up.

Serves 4

Spicy Beef and Noodle Soup

Hands-on time: 10 minutes, plus soaking
Cooking time: 10 minutes

15g (½oz) dried porcini or
    shiitake mushrooms

2 tbsp groundnut oil

225g (8oz) fillet steak, cut into
    thin strips

1.1 litres (2 pints) beef stock

2 tbsp Thai fish sauce (nam pla), plus
    extra if needed

1 large fresh red chilli, seeded and
    finely chopped (see Safety Tip,
    page 28)

1 lemongrass stalk, trimmed and
    thinly sliced

2.5cm (1in) piece of fresh root ginger,
    peeled and finely chopped

6 spring onions, halved lengthways
    and cut into 2.5cm (1in) lengths

1 garlic clove, crushed

¼ tsp caster sugar

50g (2oz) medium egg noodles

125g (4oz) fresh spinach leaves,
    roughly chopped

4 tbsp freshly chopped coriander

freshly ground black pepper

1 Break the dried mushrooms into pieces, and soak in 150ml (¼ pint) boiling water for 15 minutes.

2 Meanwhile, heat the oil in a large pan over a medium heat, brown the meat in two batches and keep to one side. Pour the stock into the pan with 2 tbsp fish sauce. Add the mushrooms and their soaking liquor, the chilli, lemongrass, ginger, spring onions, garlic and sugar. Bring to the boil.

3 Break the noodles up slightly and add to the pan, then stir gently until they begin to separate. Reduce the heat and simmer for 4–5 minutes until the noodles are just tender, stirring occasionally.

4 Stir in the spinach, coriander and reserved steak. Check and adjust the seasoning with ground black pepper, and add a little more fish sauce if necessary. Spoon into four warmed bowls and serve hot.

Serves 4

Perfect Wok

You don't need to buy special equipment to start stir-frying – a large deep-sided frying pan and a spatula will do the job – but a wok is very versatile, with many uses in the kitchen.

Choosing a wok

Traditional steel woks have rounded bottoms, so the food always returns to the centre where the heat is most intense. The deep sides prevent the food from falling out during stir-frying. Most woks now have flattened bottoms, which makes them more stable on modern hobs. Non-stick woks are widely available; they are easy to clean and not prone to rusting.

- There are two main styles of wok, one with double handles opposite each other, the other with one long handle. The double-handled wok gets very hot and needs to be handled with oven gloves, although it is slightly more stable if you use it for steaming and braising.

A wok with a long single handle is the best choice as it is easier to manipulate when stir-frying.

- A wok with a diameter of 35.5cm (14in) is most useful for cooking stir-fries for four people.
- A well-fitting lid is useful if you intend to use your wok for steaming.

Wok equipment

Wok spoon A metal utensil with a curved end to match the curve of the wok is useful for stir-frying in a traditional steel wok, but should not be used in non-stick woks – any heatproof spatula will do.

Chopsticks Long wooden chopsticks are great for stir-frying in non-stick woks; they are also useful for separating blocks of noodles as they cook.

Steamers come in various sizes, and may be of pierced metal or bamboo. They can be used in a wok or over a pan of boiling water, covered with a tight-fitting lid.

Trivet or steamer rack A wooden or metal trivet or steamer rack fits inside the wok to keep food above the water level when steaming.

Wok stand A wok stand or ring, which sits on the hob with the wok on top, helps keep the wok stable during steaming or braising.

Strainer A long-handled strainer is useful for scooping food from deep-frying oil, but a slotted spoon could be used instead.

Seasoning a wok

Non-stick woks do not need to be seasoned. Traditional steel woks, designed to withstand high temperatures, can be made practically non-stick by 'seasoning' before you use them for the first time. First scrub the wok in hot water and detergent, then dry thoroughly with kitchen paper. Place it over a low heat, add 2 tbsp groundnut oil and rub this over the entire inner surface with kitchen paper. Keep the wok over a low heat until the oil starts to smoke. Leave to cool for 5 minutes, then rub well with kitchen paper. Add another 2 tbsp oil and repeat the heating process twice more until the kitchen paper wipes clean. The wok is now seasoned. If used regularly it should remain rust-free. After each use, rinse in hot water – but not detergent – and wipe clean with kitchen paper. If you scrub your wok or use detergent you will need to season it again.

Chicken and Coconut Curry

Hands-on time: 15 minutes
Cooking time: 35 minutes

2 garlic cloves, peeled

1 onion, quartered

1 lemongrass stalk, halved

2.5cm (1in) piece fresh root ginger, peeled and halved

2 small hot chillies (see Safety Tip, page 28)

a small handful of fresh coriander

1 tsp ground coriander

grated zest and juice of 1 lime

2 tbsp vegetable oil

6 skinless chicken breast fillets, each cut into three pieces

2 large tomatoes, peeled and chopped

2 tbsp Thai fish sauce

900ml (1½ pints) coconut milk

salt and freshly ground black pepper

finely sliced red chilli to garnish (see Safety Tip, page 28)

basmati rice to serve

1 Put the garlic, onion, lemongrass, ginger, chillies, fresh coriander, ground coriander and lime zest and juice in a food processor and whiz to a paste. Add a little water if the mixture gets stuck under the blades.

2 Heat the oil in a wok or large frying pan, add the spice paste and cook over a fairly high heat for 3–4 minutes, stirring constantly. Add the chicken and cook for 5 minutes, stirring to coat in the spice mixture.

3 Add the tomatoes, fish sauce and coconut milk. Simmer, covered, for about 25 minutes or until the chicken is cooked. Season with alt and ground black pepper, garnish with red chilli and serve with basmati rice.

Serves 6

Thai Red Seafood Curry

Hands-on time: 15 minutes
Cooking time: about 10 minutes

1 tbsp vegetable oil
3 tbsp Thai red curry paste
450g (1lb) monkfish tail, boned
  to make 350g (12oz) fillet, sliced
  into rounds
350g (12oz) large raw peeled
  prawns, deveined
400ml can half-fat coconut milk
200ml (7fl oz) fish stock
juice of 1 lime
1–2 tbsp Thai fish sauce
125g (4oz) mangetouts
3 tbsp fresh coriander, roughly torn
salt and freshly ground black pepper

1 Heat the oil in a wok or large non-stick frying pan. Add the curry paste and cook for 1–2 minutes.
2 Add the monkfish and prawns and stir well to coat in the curry paste. Add the coconut milk, stock, lime juice and fish sauce. Stir all the ingredients together and bring just to the boil.
3 Add the mangetouts, reduce the heat and simmer for 5 minutes or until the mangetouts and fish are tender. Stir in the coriander and check the seasoning, adding salt and ground black pepper to taste. Serve immediately.

SAVE MONEY

If you can't find half-fat coconut milk, use half a can of full-fat coconut milk and make up the difference with water or stock. Freeze the remaining milk for up to one month.

Serves 4

Fish Curry

Hands-on time: 20 minutes
Cooking time: about 25 minutes

1 tsp vegetable oil
2 onions, finely sliced
5cm (2in) piece fresh root
  ginger, grated
1 tsp each ground turmeric
  and coriander
1 tbsp medium curry paste
4 tomatoes, roughly chopped
400ml (13fl oz) fish stock
200g (7oz) raw, peeled king prawns
300g (11oz) white skinless fish – such
  as cod, haddock, coley or pollock –
  cut into 2.5cm (1in) cubes
200g (7oz) frozen peas
salt and freshly ground black pepper
boiled rice or crusty bread to serve

1 Heat the oil in a large pan over a low heat. Add the onions and a good pinch of salt, then cover and cook for 15 minutes until completely softened. Stir in the ginger, turmeric, coriander and curry paste. Cook for 1 minute.

2 Stir in the tomatoes and stock and simmer for 5 minutes. Mix in the prawns, fish and peas, then cook for 3–5 minutes (stirring carefully to prevent the fish from breaking up) or until the prawns are bright pink and the fish is opaque. Check the seasoning and serve with rice or crusty bread, if you like.

HEALTHY TIP

If you're trying to up your vegetable intake, fold through a few large handfuls of spinach just before serving.

Serves 4

Thai Green Shellfish Curry

Hands-on time: 10 minutes
Cooking time: about 15 minutes

1 tbsp vegetable oil
1 lemongrass stalk, chopped
2 small red chillies, chopped (see Safety Tip, page 28)
a handful of fresh coriander leaves, chopped, plus extra to serve
2 kaffir lime leaves, chopped
1–2 tbsp Thai green curry paste
400ml can coconut milk
450ml (¾ pint) vegetable stock
375g (13oz) queen scallops with corals
250g (9oz) raw tiger prawns, peeled and deveined, with tails intact
salt and freshly ground black pepper
jasmine rice to serve

1 Heat the oil in a wok or large frying pan. Add the lemongrass, chillies, coriander and lime leaves and stir-fry for 30 seconds. Add the curry paste and fry for 1 minute.

2 Add the coconut milk and stock and bring to the boil. Reduce the heat and simmer for 5–10 minutes until slightly reduced. Season well with salt and ground black pepper.

3 Add the scallops and tiger prawns, bring to the boil, reduce the heat and simmer gently for 2–3 minutes until cooked. Divide the jasmine rice among six serving bowls and spoon the curry over the top. Sprinkle with coriander and serve immediately with rice.

SAVE EFFORT

For an easy alternative, use cleaned squid or mussels instead of scallops and prawns.

Thai Green Curry

Hands-on time: 10 minutes
Cooking time: 15 minutes

2 tsp vegetable oil

1 green chilli, seeded and finely chopped (see Safety Tip, page 28)

4cm (1½in) piece fresh root ginger, peeled and finely grated

1 lemongrass stalk, cut into three pieces

225g (8oz) brown-cap or oyster mushrooms

1 tbsp Thai green curry paste

300ml (½ pint) coconut milk

150ml (¼ pint) chicken stock

1 tbsp Thai fish sauce

1 tsp light soy sauce

350g (12oz) skinless chicken breast fillets, cut into bite-size pieces

350g (12oz) cooked peeled large prawns

fresh coriander sprigs to garnish

1 Heat the oil in a wok or large frying pan, add the chilli, ginger, lemongrass and mushrooms and stir-fry for about 3 minutes or until the mushrooms begin to turn golden. Add the curry paste and fry for a further 1 minute.

2 Pour in the coconut milk, stock, fish sauce and soy sauce and bring to the boil. Stir in the chicken, reduce the heat and simmer for about 8 minutes or until the chicken is cooked. Add the prawns and cook for a further 1 minute. Garnish with coriander sprigs and serve immediately.

Ginger
Grating
1 Cut off a piece of the root and peel with a vegetable peeler. Cut off any brown spots.
2 Rest the grater on a board or small plate and grate the ginger. Discard any large fibres adhering to the pulp.

Slicing, shredding and chopping
Cut slices off the ginger and cut off the skin carefully. Cut off any brown spots. Stack the slices and cut into shreds. To chop, stack the shreds of ginger and cut across into small pieces.

Pressing
If you just need the ginger juice, peel and cut off any brown spots, then cut into small chunks and use a garlic press held over a small bowl to extract the juice.

Garlic
Removing the Skin
1 Put the clove on a chopping board and place the flat side of a large knife on top of it. Press down firmly on the flat of the blade to crush the clove and break the papery skin.
2 Cut off the base of the clove and slip the garlic out of its skin. It should come away easily.

Slicing
Using a rocking motion with the knife tip on the board, slice the garlic as thinly as you need.

Shredding and chopping
Holding the slices together, shred them across the slices. Chop the shreds if you need chopped garlic.

Crushing
After step 2 above, the whole clove can be put into a garlic press. To crush with a knife: roughly chop the peeled cloves with a pinch of salt. Press down hard with the edge of a large knife tip (with the blade facing away from you), then drag the blade along the garlic while still pressing hard. Continue to do this, dragging the knife tip over the garlic.

Chillies

1 Cut off the cap and slit open lengthways. Using a spoon, scrape out the seeds and the pith.
2 For diced chilli, cut into thin shreds lengthways, then cut crossways.

Cook's Tip: Wash your hands thoroughly after handling chillies – the volatile oils will sting if accidentally rubbed into your eyes.

Coriander

Coriander, also known as Chinese parsley, is the most commonly used herb throughout Asia. In Thailand the roots are often used in curry pastes.

1 Trim off any roots and the lower part of the stalks. Immerse in cold water and shake briskly. Leave in the water for a few minutes.
2 Lift out of the water and put in a colander or sieve, then rinse again under the cold tap. Leave to drain for a few minutes, then dry thoroughly on kitchen paper or teatowels, or use a salad spinner.

Note: Don't pour the herbs and their water into the sieve, because dirt in the water might get caught in the leaves.

3 Gather the leaves into a compact ball in one hand, keeping your fist around the ball (but being careful not to crush them). Chop with a large knife, using a rocking motion and letting just a little of the ball out of your fingers at a time.
4 When the herbs are roughly chopped, continue chopping until the pieces are as fine as you need.

Lemongrass

Lemongrass is a popular Southeast Asian ingredient, giving an aromatic lemony flavour. It looks rather like a long, slender spring onion, but is fibrous and woody and is usually removed before the dish is served. Alternatively, the inner leaves may be very finely chopped or pounded in a mortar and pestle and used in spice pastes.

Thai Red Turkey Curry

Hands-on time: 20 minutes
Cooking time: about 25 minutes

3 tbsp vegetable oil
450g (1lb) onions, finely chopped
200g (7oz) green beans, trimmed
125g (4oz) baby sweetcorn, cut on
   the diagonal
2 red peppers, seeded and cut into
   thick strips
1 tbsp Thai red curry paste, or to taste
1 red chilli, seeded and finely chopped
   (see Safety Tip, page 28)
1 lemongrass stalk, very finely
   chopped
4 kaffir lime leaves, bruised
2 tbsp fresh root ginger, peeled and
   finely chopped
1 garlic clove, crushed
400ml can coconut milk
600ml (1 pint) chicken or turkey stock
450g (1lb) cooked turkey, cut
   into strips
150g (5oz) bean sprouts
fresh basil leaves to garnish

1 Heat the oil in a wok or large frying
   pan, add the onions and cook for 4–5
   minutes or until soft.

2 Add the beans, baby corn and
   peppers to the pan and stir-fry for
   3–4 minutes. Add the curry paste,
   chilli, lemongrass, kaffir lime leaves,
   ginger and garlic and cook for a
   further 2 minutes, stirring. Remove
   from the pan and put to one side.

3 Add the coconut milk and stock to
   the pan, bring to the boil and bubble
   vigorously for 5–10 minutes until
   reduced by one-quarter.

4 Put the vegetables back into the pan
   with the turkey and bean sprouts.
   Bring to the boil, reduce the heat
   and simmer for 1–2 minutes until
   heated through. Serve immediately,
   garnished with basil leaves.

SAVE MONEY

This is a great way to use
up leftover turkey.

Hot Jungle Curry

Hands-on time: 10 minutes
Cooking time: about 20 minutes

1 tbsp vegetable oil

350g (12oz) skinless chicken breast fillets, cut into 5cm (2in) strips

2 tbsp Thai red curry paste

2.5cm (1in) piece fresh root ginger, peeled and thinly sliced

125g (4oz) aubergine, cut into bite-size pieces

125g (4oz) baby sweetcorn, halved lengthways

75g (3oz) green beans, trimmed

75g (3oz) button or brown-cap mushrooms, halved if large

2–3 kaffir lime leaves (optional)

450ml (¾ pint) chicken stock

2 tbsp Thai fish sauce

grated zest of ½ lime, plus extra to garnish

1 tsp tomato purée

1 tbsp soft brown sugar

1 Heat the oil in a wok or large frying pan. Add the chicken and cook, stirring, for 5 minutes or until the chicken turns golden brown.

2 Add the red curry paste and cook for a further 1 minute. Add the ginger, aubergine, sweetcorn, beans, mushrooms and lime leaves, if you like, and stir until coated in the red curry paste. Add all the remaining ingredients and bring to the boil. Reduce the heat and simmer gently for 10–12 minutes or until the chicken and vegetables are just tender. Serve immediately, sprinkled with lime zest.

SAVE EFFORT

Add a drained 225g can of bamboo shoots with the other vegetables in step 2, if you like.

Serves 4

Lamb and Bamboo Shoot Red Curry

Hands-on time: 10 minutes
Cooking time: about 45 minutes

2 tbsp sunflower oil

1 large onion, cut into wedges

2 garlic cloves, finely chopped

450g (1lb) lean boneless lamb, cut into 3cm (1¼in) cubes

2 tbsp Thai red curry paste

150ml (¼ pint) lamb or beef stock

2 tbsp Thai fish sauce

2 tsp soft brown sugar

200g can bamboo shoots, drained and thinly sliced

1 red pepper, seeded and thinly sliced

2 tbsp freshly chopped mint

1 tbsp freshly chopped basil

25g (1oz) unsalted peanuts, toasted

boiled rice to serve

1 Heat the oil in a wok or large frying pan, add the onion and garlic and fry over a medium heat for 5 minutes.

2 Add the lamb and the curry paste and stir-fry for 5 minutes. Add the stock, fish sauce and sugar. Bring to the boil, then reduce the heat, cover and simmer gently for 20 minutes.

3 Stir the bamboo shoots, red pepper and herbs into the curry and cook, uncovered, for a further 10 minutes. Stir in the peanuts and serve immediately, with rice.

Serves 4

Thai Beef Curry

Hands-on time: 20 minutes
Cooking time: about 30 minutes, plus cooling

4 cloves

1 tsp coriander seeds

1 tsp cumin seeds

seeds from 3 cardamom pods

2 garlic cloves, roughly chopped

2.5cm (1in) piece fresh root ginger, peeled and roughly chopped

1 small onion, roughly chopped

2 tbsp sunflower oil

1 tbsp sesame oil

1 tbsp Thai red curry paste

1 tsp ground turmeric

450g (1lb) sirloin steak, cut into 3cm (1¼in) cubes

225g (8oz) potatoes, quartered

4 tomatoes, quartered

1 tsp sugar

1 tbsp light soy sauce

300ml (½ pint) coconut milk

150ml (¼ pint) beef stock

4 small red chillies, bruised (see Safety Tip, page 28)

50g (2oz) cashew nuts

boiled rice and stir-fried green vegetables to serve

1 Put the cloves, coriander, cumin and cardamom seeds in a small heavy-based frying pan and fry over a high heat for 1–2 minutes until the spices release their aroma. Be careful that they do not burn. Leave to cool slightly, then grind to a powder in a spice grinder or blender.

2 Put the garlic, ginger and onion in a blender or food processor and whiz to form a smooth paste. Heat the sunflower and sesame oils in a wok or deep frying pan. Add the onion purée and the curry paste and stir-fry for 5 minutes, then add the ground roasted spices and turmeric and fry for a further 5 minutes.

3 Add the beef to the pan and fry for 5 minutes until browned on all sides. Add the potatoes, tomatoes, sugar, soy sauce, coconut milk, stock and chillies to the pan. Bring to the boil, then reduce the heat, cover and simmer gently for about 15 minutes or until the beef is tender and the potatoes are cooked.

Serves 4

4 Stir in the cashew nuts and serve
  the curry with rice and stir-fried
  green vegetables.

Salmon Laksa Curry

Hands-on time: 10 minutes
Cooking time: about 20 minutes

1 tbsp olive oil
1 onion, thinly sliced
3 tbsp laksa paste
200ml (7fl oz) coconut milk
900ml (1½ pints) hot vegetable stock
200g (7oz) baby sweetcorn,
　halved lengthways
600g (1lb 5oz) piece skinless salmon
　fillet, cut into 1cm (½in) slices
225g (8oz) baby leaf spinach, washed
250g (9oz) medium rice noodles
salt and freshly ground black pepper
2 spring onions, sliced diagonally,
　2 tbsp freshly chopped coriander and
　1 lime, cut into wedges, to garnish

1 Heat the oil in a wok or large frying pan, then add the onion and fry over a medium heat for 10 minutes, stirring, until golden. Add the laksa paste and cook for 2 minutes.

2 Add the coconut milk, stock and baby corn and season. Bring to the boil, reduce the heat and simmer for 5 minutes.

3 Add the salmon slices and spinach, stirring to immerse them in the liquid. Cook for 4 minutes until the fish is opaque all the way through.

4 Meanwhile, put the noodles into a large heatproof bowl, pour over boiling water to cover and soak for 30 seconds. Drain well, then stir them into the curry.

5 Pour the curry into four serving bowls and garnish with the spring onions, coriander and lime wedges. Serve immediately.

SAVE EFFORT

Laksa paste is a hot and spicy paste, but you can use Thai curry paste instead.

Serves 4

Rice and Noodles

Perfect Rice

Rice is an incredibly versatile grain. Like pasta, rice is the perfect storecupboard standby. Stored in an airtight container in a cool, dry place, it has a shelf life of at least a year.

Cooking rice

There are two main types of rice: long-grain and short-grain. Long-grain rice is generally served as an accompaniment; the most commonly used type of long-grain rice in South-east Asian cooking is jasmine rice, also known as Thai fragrant rice. It has a distinctive taste and slightly sticky texture. Long-grain rice needs no special preparation, although it should be washed to remove excess starch. Put the rice in a bowl and cover with cold water. Stir until this becomes cloudy, then drain and repeat until the water is clear.

Long-grain rice

1 Use 50–75g (2–3oz) raw rice per person; measured by volume 50–75ml (2–2½fl oz). Measure the rice by volume and put it in a pan with a pinch of salt and twice the volume of boiling water (or stock).

1

2 Bring to the boil. Reduce the heat to low and set the timer for the time stated on the pack. The rice should be al dente: tender with a bite at the centre.

3 When the rice is cooked, fluff up the grains with a fork.

Basmati rice

Put the rice in a bowl and cover with cold water. Stir until this becomes cloudy, then drain and repeat until the water is clear. Soak the rice for 30 minutes, then drain before cooking.

Perfect rice

- Use 50–75g (2–3oz) raw rice per person – or measure by volume 50–75ml (2–2½fl oz).
- If you cook rice often, you may want to invest in a special rice steamer. They are available in Asian supermarkets and some kitchen shops and give good, consistent results.

Simple Fried Rice

TAKE 5

Hands-on time: 5 minutes
Cooking time: about 20 minutes

150g (5oz) long-grain rice
2 tbsp sesame oil
3 medium eggs, lightly beaten
250g (9oz) frozen petits pois
250g (9oz) cooked peeled prawns

1 Cook the rice in boiling water for about 10 minutes or according to the pack instructions. Drain well.

2 Heat 1 tsp oil in a large non-stick frying pan. Pour in half the beaten eggs and tilt the pan around over the heat for 1 minute until the egg is set. Tip the omelette on to a warmed plate. Repeat with another 1 tsp sesame oil and the remaining beaten egg to make another omelette. Tip on to another warmed plate.

3 Add the remaining oil to the pan and stir in the rice and peas. Stir-fry for 2–3 minutes until the peas are cooked. Stir in the prawns.

4 Roll up the omelettes, roughly chop one-third of one, then slice the remainder into strips. Add the chopped omelette to the rice, peas and prawns, and cook for 1–2 minutes until heated through. Divide the fried rice among four serving bowls, top with the sliced omelette and serve immediately.

Serves 4

For the slice: Onions and Peppers

Onions

1 Cut off the tip and base of the onion. Peel away all the layers of papery skin and any discoloured layers underneath.
2 Put the onion root end down on the chopping board, then, using a sharp knife, cut the onion in half from tip to base.

Slicing

Put one half on the board with the cut surface facing down and slice across the onion.

Chopping

Slice the halved onions from the root end to the top at regular intervals. Next, make two or three horizontal slices through the onion, then slice vertically across the width.

Seeding peppers

The seeds and white pith of peppers taste bitter, so should be removed.

1 Cut off the top of the pepper, then cut away and discard the seeds and white pith.
2 Alternatively, cut the pepper in half vertically and snap out the white pithy core and seeds. Trim away the rest of the white membrane with a knife.

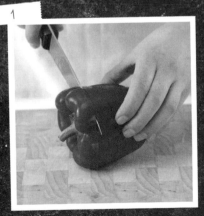

Rice and Red Pepper Stir-fry

Hands-on time: 5 minutes
Cooking time: 15 minutes

75g (3oz) long-grain rice
200ml (7fl oz) hot vegetable stock
2 tsp vegetable oil
½ onion, thinly sliced
2 rashers of streaky bacon, chopped
1 small red pepper, seeded and cut
  into chunks
a handful of frozen peas
a dash of Worcestershire sauce

1 Put the rice in a pan and pour over the hot stock. Cover, bring to the boil, reduce the heat and simmer for 10 minutes or until the rice is tender and the liquid has been absorbed.

2 Meanwhile, heat the oil in a wok or large frying pan over a medium heat. Add the onion and fry for 5 minutes. Add the bacon and pepper and fry for a further 5 minutes or until the bacon is crisp.

3 Stir the cooked rice and the peas into the onion mixture and cook, stirring occasionally, for 2–3 minutes until the rice and peas are hot. Add a dash of Worcestershire sauce and serve immediately.

Serves 4

Special Prawn Fried Rice

Hands-on time: 5 minutes
Cooking time: about 13 minutes

1 tbsp sesame oil
6 tbsp nasi goreng paste
200g (7oz) green cabbage, shredded
250g (9oz) cooked peeled
  large prawns
2 × 250g packs microwave rice
2 tbsp light soy sauce
1 tbsp sunflower oil
2 medium eggs, beaten
2 spring onions, thinly sliced
1 lime, cut into wedges, to serve

SAVE MONEY

If you prefer not to use
microwave rice, use 200g
(7oz) long-grain rice, cooked
according to the pack
instructions – but do not
overcook. Rinse the rice in cold
water and drain well before you
begin the recipe.

1 Heat the sesame oil in a wok and fry the nasi goreng paste for 1–2 minutes. Add the cabbage and stir-fry for 2–3 minutes. Add the prawns and stir briefly, then add the rice and soy sauce and cook for a further 5 minutes, stirring occasionally.

2 To make the omelette, heat the sunflower oil in a non-stick frying pan (about 25.5cm/10in in diameter) and add the eggs. Swirl around to cover the base of the pan in a thin layer and cook for 2–3 minutes until set.

3 Roll up the omelette and cut it into strips. Serve the rice scattered with the omelette and spring onions, and pass around the lime wedges to squeeze over.

Serves 4

Yellow Bean Noodles with Tiger Prawns

Hands-on time: 10 minutes, plus soaking
Cooking time: 5 minutes

250g (9oz) medium egg noodles
1 tbsp stir-fry oil or sesame oil
1 garlic clove, sliced
1 tsp freshly grated root ginger
1 bunch of spring onions, each
   cut into four
250g (9oz) raw peeled tiger prawns,
   thawed if frozen
200g (7oz) pak choi, leaves separated
   and white base cut into thick slices
160g jar Chinese yellow bean
   stir-fry sauce

1 Put the noodles into a large
   heatproof bowl and pour over
   2 litres (3½ pints) boiling water.
   Leave to soak for 4 minutes. Drain
   and put to one side.

2 Heat the oil in a wok or large frying
   pan. Add the garlic and ginger,
   then stir-fry for 30 seconds. Add the
   spring onions and prawns and cook
   for 2 minutes.

3 Boil the kettle. Add the sliced white
   pak choi stems to the pan with the
   yellow bean sauce. Fill the sauce jar
   with boiling water, pour it into the
   pan and stir well to mix.

4 Add the drained noodles to the
   pan and cook for 1 minute, tossing
   every now and then, until heated
   through. Stir in the pak choi leaves
   and serve immediately.

SAVE EFFORT

For an easy alternative, use
chicken, cut into thin strips,
instead of the prawns.

Serves 4

Perfect Noodles

Noodles, along with rice, are one of the staples of Asian cooking. Often served as an accompaniment to stir-fried dishes, they can also be cooked and added as one of the ingredients.

Cooking noodles
Egg (wheat) noodles

These are the most versatile of Asian noodles. Like Italian pasta, they are made from wheat flour, egg and water and are available fresh or dried in various thicknesses.

1 Bring a pan of water to the boil and put the noodles in.
2 Agitate the noodles using chopsticks or a fork to separate them. This can take a minute or even more.
3 Continue boiling for 4–5 minutes until the noodles are cooked al dente: tender but with a little bite in the centre.
4 Drain well and then rinse in cold water and toss with a little oil if you are not planning to use them immediately.

Glass, cellophane or bean thread noodles

These very thin noodles are made from mung beans; they need only 1 minute in boiling water.

Rice noodles

These may be very fine (rice vermicelli) or thick and flat. Most need no cooking, only soaking in warm or hot water; check the pack instructions, or cover the noodles with freshly boiled water and soak until they are al dente: tender but with a little bite in the centre. Drain well and toss with a little oil if you are not using them immediately.

Perfect noodles

- Use 50–75g (2–3oz) uncooked noodles per person.
- Dried egg noodles are often packed in layers. As a general rule, allow one layer per person for a main dish.
- If you plan to re-cook the noodles after the initial boiling or soaking – for example, in a stir-fry – it's best to undercook them slightly.
- When cooking a layer, block or nest of noodles, use a pair of forks or chopsticks to untangle the strands from the moment the noodles go into the water.

Thai Noodles with Tofu

Hands-on time: 25 minutes
Cooking time: 35 minutes

125g (4oz) firm tofu, drained and cut
   into 2.5cm (1in) cubes
8 shallots, halved
1 garlic clove, crushed
2.5cm (1in) piece fresh root ginger,
   peeled and grated
2 tbsp soy sauce
1 tsp rice vinegar
225g (8oz) rice noodles
25g (1oz) unsalted peanuts
2 tbsp sunflower oil
15g (½oz) dried shrimp (optional)
1 medium egg, beaten
25g (1oz) bean sprouts
fresh basil leaves to garnish

For the sauce:

1 dried red chilli, seeded and
   finely chopped
2 tbsp lemon juice
1 tbsp Thai fish sauce
1 tbsp caster sugar
2 tbsp smooth peanut butter

1 Preheat the oven to 200°C (180°C
fan oven) mark 6. Put the tofu and
shallots into a small roasting pan.
Put the garlic, ginger, soy sauce,
vinegar and 2 tbsp water in a bowl
and stir well. Pour the mixture over
the tofu and shallots and toss well
to coat. Roast near the top of the
oven for 30 minutes until the tofu
and shallots are golden.

2 Meanwhile, soak the noodles
according to the pack instructions.
Drain, refresh under cold running
water and put to one side. Toast and
chop the peanuts.

3 To make the sauce, put all the
ingredients in a small pan and stir
over a gentle heat until the sugar
dissolves. Keep the sauce warm.

4 Heat the oil in a wok or large frying
pan and stir-fry the dried shrimp,
if you like, for 1 minute. Add the
drained noodles and beaten egg
to the pan and stir over a medium
heat for 3 minutes. Add the tofu

Serves 4

and shallots, together with any pan juices. Stir well, then remove from the heat.

5 Stir in the bean sprouts and the sauce, then divide among four warmed serving plates. Sprinkle with the toasted peanuts and serve immediately, garnished with fresh basil leaves.

Quick Pad Thai

Hands-on time: 12 minutes, plus soaking
Cooking time: 8 minutes

250g (9oz) wide ribbon rice noodles
3 tbsp each of satay and sweet
  chilli pesto
125g (4oz) mangetouts, thinly sliced
125g (4oz) sugarsnap peas,
  thinly sliced
3 medium eggs, beaten
3 tbsp chilli soy sauce, plus extra
  to serve
250g (9oz) cooked peeled tiger prawns
25g (1oz) dry-roasted peanuts,
  roughly crushed
lime wedges to serve (optional)

SAVE EFFORT

If you can't find satay and sweet
chilli pesto, substitute 2 tbsp
peanut butter and 1 tbsp sweet
chilli sauce. Chilli soy sauce can
be replaced with 2 tbsp light soy
sauce and ½ red chilli, finely
chopped (see Safety Tip, page 28).

1 Put the noodles in a heatproof bowl, cover with boiling water and soak for 4 minutes until softened. Drain, rinse under cold water and put to one side.

2 Heat a wok or large frying pan until hot, add the satay and chilli pesto and stir-fry for 1 minute. Add the mangetouts and sugarsnap peas and cook for a further 2 minutes. Tip into a bowl. Put the pan back on the heat, add the eggs and cook, stirring, for 1 minute.

3 Add the soy sauce, prawns and noodles to the pan. Toss well and cook for 3 minutes until piping hot. Put the vegetables back into the pan, cook for a further 1 minute until heated through, then sprinkle with the peanuts. Serve with extra soy sauce and lime wedges to squeeze over, if you like.

Serves 4

Pork and Noodle Stir-fry

Hands-on time: 15 minutes, plus marinating
Cooking time: about 8 minutes

1 tbsp sesame oil

5cm (2in) piece fresh root ginger,
  peeled and grated

2 tbsp soy sauce

1 tbsp fish sauce

½ red chilli, finely chopped (see Safety
  Tip, page 28)

450g (1lb) stir-fry pork strips

2 red peppers, seeded and
  roughly chopped

250g (9oz) baby sweetcorn,
  halved lengthways

200g (7oz) sugarsnap peas, halved

300g (11oz) bean sprouts

250g (9oz) rice noodles

1 Put the oil in a large bowl. Add the ginger, soy sauce, fish sauce, chilli and pork strips. Mix well and leave to marinate for 10 minutes.

2 Heat a wok or large frying pan until hot. Lift the pork out of the marinade with a slotted spoon and add it to the pan. Stir-fry over a high heat for 5 minutes. Add the peppers, sweetcorn, sugarsnap peas, bean sprouts and remaining marinade and stir-fry for a further 2–3 minutes until the pork is cooked.

3 Meanwhile, soak the noodles for 4 minutes or according to the pack instructions.

4 Drain the noodles, add them to the pan and toss well. Serve immediately.

Serves 4

Chicken Chow Mein

Hands-on time: 10 minutes
Cooking time: 10 minutes

250g (9oz) medium egg noodles

1 tbsp toasted sesame oil

2 skinless chicken breast fillets,
cut into thin strips

a bunch of spring onions, thinly
sliced diagonally

150g (5oz) mangetouts, thickly
sliced diagonally

125g (4oz) bean sprouts

100g (3½oz) cooked ham,
finely shredded

120g sachet chow mein sauce

salt and freshly ground black pepper

light soy sauce to serve

1 Cook the noodles in boiling water
for 4 minutes or according to the
pack instructions. Drain, rinse
thoroughly in cold water, drain and
put to one side.

2 Meanwhile, heat a wok or large
frying pan until hot, then add the
oil. Add the chicken and stir-fry over
a high heat for 3–4 minutes until
browned all over. Add the spring
onions and mangetouts, stir-fry
for 2 minutes, then stir in the bean
sprouts and ham and cook for a
further 2 minutes.

3 Add the drained noodles, then pour
over the chow mein sauce and toss
together to coat evenly. Stir-fry for
2 minutes or until piping hot. Season
with salt and ground black pepper
and serve immediately with light
soy sauce to drizzle over.

Quick Chicken Stir-fry

Hands-on time: 10 minutes
Cooking time: 12 minutes

1 tsp groundnut oil

300g (11oz) boneless, skinless chicken breasts, sliced

4 spring onions, chopped

200g (7oz) medium rice noodles

100g (3½oz) mangetouts

200g (7oz) purple sprouting broccoli, chopped

2–3 tbsp sweet chilli sauce

coriander leaves to garnish

lime wedges (optional) to serve

1 Heat the oil in a wok or large frying pan. Add the chicken and spring onions and stir-fry over a high heat for 5–6 minutes until the chicken is golden brown.

2 Meanwhile, soak the rice noodles in boiling water for 4 minutes or according to the pack instructions.

3 Add the mangetouts, broccoli and chilli sauce to the chicken. Continue to stir-fry for 4 minutes.

4 Drain the noodles, then add to the pan and toss everything together. Scatter the coriander over the top and serve with lime wedges to squeeze over the stir-fry, if you like.

SAVE EFFORT

Other vegetables are just as good in this dish: try pak choi, button mushrooms, carrots cut into matchsticks, or baby sweetcorn.

Serves 4

Beef Chow Mein

Hands-on time: 15 minutes, plus marinating
Cooking time: 15 minutes

2 tsp dark soy sauce

4 tsp dry sherry

1 tsp cornflour

1 tsp sugar

1 tbsp sesame oil

225g (8oz) rump steak, cut into thin strips about 7.5cm (3in) long

175g (6oz) egg noodles

3 tbsp vegetable oil

1 bunch of spring onions, sliced

3 garlic cloves, crushed

1 large green chilli, sliced (see Safety Tip, page 28)

125g (4oz) Chinese leaves, or cabbage, sliced

50g (2oz) bean sprouts

salt and freshly ground black pepper

1 Put the soy sauce, sherry, cornflour, sugar and 1 tsp sesame oil in a bowl and whisk together. Pour this mixture over the beef. Cover and marinate in the fridge for at least 1 hour or overnight.

2 Cook the noodles for 4 minutes or according to the pack instructions. Rinse in cold water and drain.

3 Drain the beef, keeping the marinade to one side. Heat the vegetable oil in a wok or large, non-stick frying pan and fry the beef over a high heat until well browned. Remove with a slotted spoon and put to one side.

4 Add the spring onions, garlic, chilli, Chinese leaves and bean sprouts to the pan and stir-fry for 2–3 minutes. Put the beef back into the pan with the noodles and reserved marinade. Bring to the boil, stirring all the time, and bubble for 2–3 minutes. Sprinkle over the remaining sesame oil, season and serve immediately.

Serves 4

Mee Goreng

Hands-on time: 30 minutes
Cooking time: about 12 minutes

125g (4oz) rump steak, very thinly sliced across the grain

2 garlic cloves

2 tbsp soy sauce

450g (1lb) cleaned squid

225g (8oz) egg noodles

1 tbsp vegetable oil

1 tbsp sesame oil

1–2 hot red chillies, chopped (see Safety Tip, page 28)

2.5cm (1in) piece fresh root ginger, peeled and finely chopped

2–3 spring onions, sliced

175g (6oz) large raw peeled prawns, deveined

2 tbsp hoisin sauce

1 tbsp lemon juice

2 tbsp Thai fish sauce

125g (4oz) bean sprouts

1 medium egg, beaten

lemon wedges to serve

1 Put the steak in a shallow dish with 1 garlic clove and 1 tbsp soy sauce. Leave to stand.

2 Wash and dry the squid. Cut the tentacles into small pieces. Open out the body pouches and cut into small rectangular pieces.

3 Put the noodles in a large heatproof bowl and pour over plenty of boiling water. Leave to soak for about 4 minutes or according to the pack instructions.

4 Heat the vegetable and sesame oils in a wok or large frying pan, add the remaining garlic, the chillies, ginger and spring onions and cook for 2 minutes, stirring all the time.

5 Add the beef and cook for 2 minutes. Add the squid and prawns and cook for 2 minutes. Add the hoisin sauce, lemon juice, fish sauce and remaining soy sauce and cook for 2 minutes.

6 Drain the noodles and add them to the pan with the bean sprouts. Cook for 2 minutes until heated through, then add the beaten egg. Cook briefly until the egg is on the point of setting. Serve with lemon wedges.

Serves 6

Veggie Dishes

Summer Vegetable Stir-fry

Hands-on time: 15 minutes
Cooking time: about 8 minutes

125g (4oz) baby carrots, scrubbed and trimmed

1 tbsp sesame seeds

2 tbsp sunflower oil

2 garlic cloves, roughly chopped

125g (4oz) baby courgettes, halved lengthways

1 large yellow pepper, seeded and cut into thick strips

125g (4oz) thin asparagus spears, trimmed

125g (4oz) cherry tomatoes, halved

2 tbsp balsamic or sherry vinegar

1 tsp sesame oil

salt and freshly ground black pepper

HEALTHY TIP

Vary the vegetables, but always blanch the harder ones first. For a winter vegetable stir-fry, use cauliflower and broccoli florets, carrot sticks, 2–3 sliced spring onions and a little chopped fresh root ginger.

1 Blanch the baby carrots in boiling salted water for 2 minutes, then drain and pat dry.

2 Toast the sesame seeds in a hot dry wok or large frying pan over a medium heat, stirring until they turn golden. Tip on to a plate.

3 Put the wok or frying pan back on to the heat, add the sunflower oil and heat until it is smoking. Add the chopped garlic to the oil and stir-fry for 20 seconds. Add the carrots, courgettes, yellow pepper and asparagus. Stir-fry over a high heat for 1 minute.

4 Add the cherry tomatoes and season to taste. Stir-fry for 3–4 minutes until the vegetables are just tender. Add the vinegar and sesame oil, toss well and sprinkle with the toasted sesame seeds. Serve immediately.

Serves 4

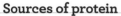

Sources of protein

Most vegetarians needn't worry about getting enough protein: this nutrient is found in a wide variety of foods including pulses, tofu and other soya bean products, Quorn, eggs, cheese, and sprouted beans and seeds.

Pulses

The term 'pulse' is used to describe all the various beans, peas and lentils. Pulses are highly nutritious, especially when eaten with grains such as couscous, pasta, rice or bread. Dried pulses should be stored in airtight containers in a cool, dry cupboard. They keep well, but after about six months their skins start to toughen and they take progressively longer to cook. Most pulses must be soaked prior to cooking. Canned pulses are a convenient, quick alternative to having to soak and cook dried ones, and most supermarkets stock a wide range. A 400g can (drained weight about 235g) is roughly equivalent to 100g (3½oz) dried beans. Dried pulses double in weight after soaking.

Sprouted beans and seeds

These are rich in nutrients and lend a nutty taste and crunchy texture to salads and stir-fries. Fresh bean sprouts are available from most supermarkets. Many beans and seeds can be sprouted at home, though it is important to buy ones that are specifically produced for sprouting – from a health food shop or other reliable source. Mung beans, aduki beans, alfalfa seeds and fenugreek are all suitable.

Cheese

Some vegetarians prefer to avoid cheeses that have been produced by the traditional method, because this uses animal-derived rennet. Most supermarkets and cheese shops now stock an excellent range of vegetarian cheeses, produced using vegetarian rennet that comes from plants such as thistle and mallow, which contain enzymes capable of curdling milk.

Tofu

Also known as bean curd, tofu is made from ground soya beans in a process akin to cheese-making. It is highly nutritious but virtually tasteless. However, it readily absorbs other flavours when marinated.

Tofu is sold as a chilled product and should be stored in the fridge. Once the pack is opened, the tofu should be kept immersed in a bowl of water in the fridge and eaten within four days.

Firm tofu is usually cut into chunks, then immersed in tasty marinades or dressings prior to grilling, stir-frying, deep-frying, adding to stews, or tossing raw into salads.

It can also be chopped and made into burgers and nut roasts. Smoked tofu has more flavour than unsmoked; it is used in the same way but doesn't need marinating. Silken tofu is softer and creamier than firm tofu and is useful for making sauces and dressings.

Textured vegetable protein (TVP)

TVP forms the bulk of most ready-prepared vegetarian burgers, sausages and mince. It is made from a mixture of soya flour, flavourings and liquid, which is cooked, then extruded under pressure and cut into chunks or small pieces to resemble mince. It has a slightly chewy, meat-like texture. TVP can be included in stews, pies, curries and other dishes, rather as meat would be used by non-vegetarians.

Quorn

Quorn is a vegetarian product derived from a distant relative of the mushroom. Although it is not suitable for vegans because it contains egg albumen, Quorn is a good source of complete protein for vegetarians. Like tofu, Quorn has a bland flavour and benefits from being marinated before cooking. Find it in the chiller cabinet at the supermarket, and keep it in the fridge.

Sweet Chilli Tofu Stir-fry

Hands-on time: 5 minutes, plus marinating
Cooking time: 12 minutes

200g (7oz) firm tofu

4 tbsp sweet chilli sauce

2 tbsp light soy sauce

1 tbsp sesame seeds

2 tbsp toasted sesame oil

600g (1lb 5oz) ready-prepared
   mixed stir-fry vegetables, such
   as carrots, broccoli, mangetouts
   and bean sprouts

a handful of pea shoots or young salad
   leaves to garnish

1 Drain the tofu, pat it dry and cut it into large cubes. Put the tofu in a shallow container and pour over 1 tbsp sweet chilli sauce and 1 tbsp light soy sauce. Cover and marinate for 10 minutes.

2 Meanwhile, toast the sesame seeds in a hot wok or large frying pan until golden. Tip on to a plate.

3 Put the wok or frying pan back on to the heat and add 1 tbsp sesame oil. Add the marinated tofu and stir-fry for 5 minutes until golden. Remove and put to one side.

4 Heat the remaining 1 tbsp oil in the pan, add the vegetables and stir-fry for 3–4 minutes until just tender. Stir in the cooked tofu.

5 Pour the remaining sweet chilli sauce and soy sauce into the pan, toss well and cook for a further 1 minute until heated through. Sprinkle with the toasted sesame seeds and pea shoots or salad leaves and serve immediately.

Serves 4

Stir-fried Vegetables with Oyster Sauce

Hands-on time: 20 minutes
Cooking time: about 10 minutes

175g (6oz) firm tofu

vegetable oil to shallow- and deep-fry

2 garlic cloves, thinly sliced

1 green pepper, seeded and sliced

225g (8oz) broccoli, cut into small florets

125g (4oz) green beans, trimmed and halved

50g (2oz) bean sprouts

50g (2oz) canned straw mushrooms, drained

125g (4oz) canned water chestnuts, drained

fresh coriander sprigs to garnish

For the sauce:

100ml (3½fl oz) vegetable stock

2 tbsp oyster sauce

1 tbsp light soy sauce

2 tsp clear honey

1 tsp cornflour

a pinch of salt

1 First, make the sauce. Put all the ingredients in a blender and blend until smooth. Put to one side.

2 Drain the tofu, pat it dry and cut it into large cubes. Heat the vegetable oil in a deep-fryer to 180°C (test by frying a small cube of bread; it should brown in 40 seconds). Add the tofu and deep-fry for 1–2 minutes until golden. Drain on kitchen paper.

3 Heat 2 tbsp oil in a wok or large frying pan, add the garlic and fry for 1 minute. Remove the garlic with a slotted spoon and discard. Add the pepper, broccoli and beans to the oil in the pan and stir-fry for 3 minutes. Add the bean sprouts, mushrooms and water chestnuts and stir-fry for a further 1 minute.

4 Add the tofu and sauce to the pan and simmer, covered, for 3–4 minutes. Garnish with coriander sprigs and serve immediately.

Serves 4

Tofu Noodle Curry

Hands-on time: 15 minutes, plus marinating
Cooking time: about 25 minutes

250g (9oz) firm tofu

2 tbsp light soy sauce

½ red chilli, chopped (see Safety Tip, page 28)

5cm (2in) piece fresh root ginger, peeled and grated

1 tbsp olive oil

1 onion, thinly sliced

2 tbsp Thai red curry paste

200ml (7fl oz) coconut milk

900ml (1½ pints) hot vegetable stock

200g (7oz) baby sweetcorn, halved lengthways

200g (7oz) fine green beans, trimmed

250g (9oz) medium rice noodles

salt and freshly ground black pepper

2 spring onions, sliced diagonally, fresh coriander sprigs and 1 lime, cut into wedges, to garnish

1 Drain the tofu, pat it dry and cut it into large cubes. Put the tofu in a large shallow bowl with the soy sauce, chilli and ginger. Toss well to coat, then leave to marinate for 30 minutes.

2 Heat the oil in a wok or large frying pan, then add the onion and fry over a medium heat for 10 minutes, stirring, until golden. Add the curry paste and cook for 2 minutes.

3 Add the marinated tofu, coconut milk, stock and baby corn and season with salt and ground black pepper. Bring to the boil, then add the green beans. Reduce the heat and simmer for 8–10 minutes.

4 Meanwhile, put the noodles into a large heatproof bowl, pour over boiling water to cover and soak for 30 seconds. Drain, then stir the noodles into the curry.

5 Pour the curry into four serving bowls and garnish with the spring onions, coriander and lime wedges. Serve immediately.

Serves 4

Aubergines in a Hot Sweet and Sour Sauce

Hands-on time: 10 minutes
Cooking time: 35 minutes

3 tbsp vegetable oil

200g (7oz) onions, thinly sliced

2.5cm (1in) piece fresh root ginger, peeled and finely chopped

2 red chillies, finely chopped, plus extra whole red chillies (see Safety Tip, page 28) to garnish (optional)

1½ tsp cumin seeds

1½ tsp coriander seeds

3 cloves

5cm (2in) cinnamon stick

1 tbsp paprika

juice of 2 limes

3–4 tbsp dark muscovado sugar

1–2 tsp salt

450g (1lb) aubergines, cut into 2.5cm (1in) pieces

boiled rice to serve

1 Heat the oil in a wok or large frying pan, add the onions, ginger and chillies and stir-fry for about 4 minutes until softened. Add the cumin and coriander seeds, cloves and cinnamon stick and cook for 2–3 minutes.

2 Add 300ml (½ pint) water to the pan, then stir in the paprika, lime juice, sugar, salt and aubergines. Bring to the boil, then reduce the heat and simmer, covered, for about 20 minutes until the aubergine is tender.

3 Uncover the pan and bring the sauce back to the boil. Bubble for 3–4 minutes until the liquid is thick enough to coat the aubergine pieces. Serve with rice, garnished with whole red chillies if you like.

Serves 4

Growing Your Own Sprouted Beans

Mung beans are the most commonly used sprouted beans for stir-fries, but chickpeas, green or Puy lentils and alfalfa are equally good and easy for home sprouting.

Sprouting beans

You will only need about 3 tbsp beans to sprout at one time.

1. Pick through the beans to remove any grit or stones, then soak in cold water for at least 8 hours. Drain and place in a clean (preferably sterilised) jar. Cover the top with a dampened piece of clean cloth, secure and leave in a warm, dark place.

2 Rinse the sprouting beans twice
a day. The sprouts can be eaten
when there is about 1cm (½in)
of growth, or they can be left
to grow for a day or two longer.
When they are sprouted, leave
the jar on a sunny windowsill for
about 3 hours – this will improve
both their flavour and their
nutrients. Then rinse and
dry them well. They can be
kept for about three days in
the fridge.

2

Bean Sprouts with Peppers and Chillies

Hands-on time: 10 minutes
Cooking time: 5 minutes

3 tbsp vegetable oil

2 garlic cloves, chopped

2.5cm (1in) piece fresh root ginger, peeled and chopped

6 spring onions, cut into 2.5cm (1in) pieces

1 red pepper, seeded and thinly sliced

1 yellow pepper, seeded and thinly sliced

2 green chillies, seeded and finely chopped (see Safety Tip, page 28)

350g (12oz) bean sprouts

1 tbsp dark soy sauce

1 tbsp sugar

1 tbsp malt vinegar

a few drops of sesame oil (optional)

boiled rice with 2 tbsp freshly chopped coriander stirred through to serve

1 Heat the oil in a wok or large frying pan. Add the garlic, ginger, spring onions, peppers, chillies and bean sprouts and stir-fry over a medium heat for 3 minutes.

2 Add the soy sauce, sugar and vinegar and fry, stirring, for a further 1 minute.

3 Sprinkle with a few drops of sesame oil, if you like, then serve immediately with coriander rice.

SAVE MONEY

Grow your own bean sprouts for this recipe following the technique on pages 106–107.

Serves 4

Egg Fu Yung

Hands-on time: 10 minutes
Cooking time: about 5 minutes

3 tbsp groundnut or vegetable oil
8 spring onions, finely sliced, plus
   spring onion curls (see Save Effort,
   page 144) to garnish
125g (4oz) shiitake or oyster
   mushrooms, sliced
125g (4oz) canned bamboo shoots,
   drained and chopped
½ green pepper, seeded and
   finely chopped
125g (4oz) frozen peas, thawed
6 medium eggs, beaten
2 good pinches of chilli powder
1 tbsp light soy sauce
a pinch of salt

1 Heat the oil in a wok or large
  frying pan, add the spring onions,
  mushrooms, bamboo shoots,
  green pepper and peas and stir-fry
  for 2–3 minutes.
2 Season the eggs with salt and chilli
  powder. Pour the eggs into the pan
  and continue to cook, stirring, until
  the egg mixture is set.
3 Sprinkle over the soy sauce and stir
  well. Serve immediately, garnished
  with spring onion curls.

Vegetable Fried Rice

Hands-on time: 10 minutes, plus soaking and chilling
Cooking time: about 30 minutes, plus cooling

200g (7oz) long-grain rice
3 Chinese dried mushrooms, or 125g (4oz) button mushrooms, sliced
2 tbsp vegetable oil
4 spring onions, sliced diagonally into 2.5cm (1in) lengths
125g (4oz) canned bamboo shoots, drained and cut into 2.5cm (1in) strips
125g (4oz) bean sprouts
125g (4oz) frozen peas
2 tbsp soy sauce
3 medium eggs, beaten
fresh coriander sprigs to garnish

1 Put the rice in a pan, cover with enough cold water to come 2.5cm (1in) above the rice, bring to the boil, cover tightly, reduce the heat and simmer very gently for 20 minutes. Do not stir.

2 Remove the pan from the heat, leave to cool for 20 minutes, then cover with clingfilm and chill for 2–3 hours or overnight.

3 When ready to fry the rice, soak the dried mushrooms, if you like, in warm water for about 30 minutes.

4 Drain the mushrooms, squeeze out excess moisture, then thinly slice.

5 Heat the oil in a wok or large frying pan over a high heat. Add the mushrooms, spring onions, bamboo shoots, bean sprouts and peas and stir-fry for 2–3 minutes. Add the soy sauce and cook briefly, stirring.

6 Fork up the rice, add it to the pan and stir-fry for 2 minutes. Pour in the eggs and continue to stir-fry for 2–3 minutes until the egg has scrambled and the rice is heated through. Serve immediately, garnished with coriander.

Serves 4

Crispy Noodles with Hot Sweet and Sour Sauce

Hands-on time: 10 minutes
Cooking time: about 15 minutes

vegetable oil to deep-fry

125g (4oz) rice or egg noodles

frisée leaves to serve

For the sauce:

2 tbsp vegetable oil

1 garlic clove, crushed

1cm (½in) piece fresh root ginger, peeled and grated

6 spring onions, sliced

½ red pepper, seeded and finely chopped

2 tbsp sugar

2 tbsp malt vinegar

2 tbsp tomato ketchup

2 tbsp dark soy sauce

2 tbsp dry sherry

1 tbsp cornflour

1 tbsp sliced green chillies (see Safety Tip, page 28)

1 First, make the sauce. Heat the oil in a wok or large frying pan and stir-fry the garlic, ginger, spring onions and red pepper for 1 minute. Stir in the sugar, vinegar, ketchup, soy sauce and sherry. Blend the cornflour with 8 tbsp water and stir it into the sauce. Cook for 2 minutes, stirring. Add the chillies, cover and keep the sauce warm.

2 Heat the vegetable oil in a deep-fryer to 190°C (test by frying a small cube of bread; it should brown in 20 seconds). Cut the noodles into six portions and fry, a batch at a time, very briefly until lightly golden (take care as the hot oil rises up quickly).

3 Drain the noodles on kitchen paper and keep them warm while you cook the remainder.

4 Arrange the noodles on a bed of frisée leaves and serve immediately with the sauce served separately.

Serves 4

Fish and Seafood

Chilli Crab Noodles

Hands-on time: 10 minutes
Cooking time: about 15 minutes

200g (7oz) medium egg noodles
1 tbsp vegetable oil
400g (14oz) frozen mixed vegetables
6 tbsp sweet chilli sauce
1 tbsp soy sauce
½ tbsp cornflour
100ml (3½fl oz) chicken or
  vegetable stock
170g canned crab, drained
frozen or freshly chopped coriander
  leaves, (optional)

1 Bring a pan of water to the boil and cook the noodles according to the pack instructions. Drain well and put to one side.

2 Heat the oil in a large wok until smoking. Add the mixed vegetables and stir-fry for 5 minutes or until piping hot.

3 In a small bowl, stir together the sweet chilli sauce, soy sauce, cornflour and stock. Add the sauce to the wok; bubble for 1 minute, then toss through the noodles, crab and coriander, if you like. Check the seasoning and serve immediately.

SAVE EFFORT

If you don't have canned crab, any canned fish or fresh or frozen seafood would work just as well.

Serves 4

Perfect Scallops

Scallops are a delicately flavoured shellfish, contained within shells
that can be a little tricky to open. Ask your fishmonger to prepare them
if you prefer. The fish themselves have a marvellous taste.

Opening scallops

Scallops can be eaten raw, either
seasoned or marinated in citrus
juice with seasonings. They take
very little cooking, usually between
5 and 10 minutes.

1 Hold the scallop with the flat
   half of the shell facing up. Firmly
   ease a very sharp small knife
   between the shells at a point
   close to the hinge.

1

2 Keeping the knife angled towards the flat shell, cut all along the shell surface until the two shells can be separated easily. Cut along the bottom of the rounded shell to release its contents. Cut loose the meat and the grey/orange coral and discard everything else.

3 Rinse off any grit, cut the coral from the round meat, and cut the little scrap of muscle from the edge of the meat.

Cooking scallops

Gently poach the white meat in wine for 5 minutes, then add the coral and simmer for 5 minutes. Sauté until crisp on the outside. Sear briefly on each side in a very hot pan until the surface browns and the inside remains tender. Thread on to skewers and grill. Bake in the shell with a sauce.

2

Scallops with Ginger

Hands-on time: 15 minutes
Cooking time: 3 minutes

2 tbsp vegetable oil
500g (1lb 2oz) shelled large scallops,
  cut into 5mm (¼in) slices
4 celery sticks, sliced diagonally
1 bunch of spring onions,
  sliced diagonally
25g (1oz) piece fresh root ginger,
  peeled and sliced
2 large garlic cloves, sliced
¼ tsp chilli powder
2 tbsp lemon juice
2 tbsp light soy sauce
3 tbsp freshly chopped coriander
salt and freshly ground black pepper

1 Heat the oil in a wok or large frying pan. Add the scallops, celery, spring onions, ginger, garlic and chilli powder and stir-fry over a high heat for 2 minutes or until the vegetables are just tender.

2 Pour in the lemon juice and soy sauce, allow to bubble up, then stir in about 2 tbsp chopped coriander and season with salt and ground black pepper. Serve immediately sprinkled with the remaining chopped coriander.

Serves 4

Perfect Mussels

One of the most popular shellfish, mussels takes moments to cook. Careful preparation is important, so give yourself enough time to get the shellfish ready.

Preparing mussels

1. Scrape off the fibres attached to the shells (beards). If the mussels are very clean, give them a quick rinse under the cold tap. If they are very sandy, scrub them with a stiff brush.

2. If the shells have sizeable barnacles on them, it is best (though not essential) to remove them. Rap them sharply with a metal spoon or the back of a washing-up brush, then scrape off.

Cooking mussels

1. Discard any open mussels that don't shut when sharply tapped; this means they are dead and could be dangerous to eat.

2. In a large heavy-based pan, fry 2 finely chopped shallots and a generous handful of parsley in 25g (1oz) butter for about 2 minutes or until soft. Pour in 1cm (½in) dry white wine.

3. Add the mussels to the pan and cover tightly with a lid. Steam for 5-10 minutes until the shells open. Immediately take the pan away from the heat.

4. Using a slotted spoon, remove the mussels from the pan and discard any that haven't opened, then boil the cooking liquid rapidly to reduce. Pour over the mussels and serve immediately.

2

3

Thai Coconut Mussels

Hands-on time: 15 minutes
Cooking time: about 12 minutes

1 tbsp vegetable oil
2 shallots, finely chopped
2-3 tbsp Thai green curry paste
400ml can coconut milk
2kg (4½lb) mussels, scrubbed and
   beards removed
a small handful of fresh coriander,
   chopped, plus extra sprigs
   to garnish

1 Heat the oil in a large, deep pan.
  Add the shallots and curry paste
  and fry gently for 5 minutes, stirring
  regularly, until the shallots are
  starting to soften. Stir in the coconut
  milk, cover with a tight-fitting lid
  and bring to the boil.
2 Add the mussels to the pan, cover,
  shake the pan well and cook over a
  medium heat for 4-5 minutes. Give
  the pan another good shake. Check
  the mussels and discard any that
  are still closed. Stir in the chopped
  coriander and serve immediately,
  garnished with coriander sprigs.

SAVE EFFORT

For an easy alternative, instead
of mussels you could use 500g
(1lb 2oz) large raw peeled prawns;
simmer for 5 minutes until the
prawns are cooked and pink.

Serves 4

Perfect Prawns

Prawns, mussels and small squid are ideal for stir-frying and quick braising, because they need very brief cooking, otherwise they will become rubbery in texture.

Peeling and butterflying

1 To peel prawns, pull off the head and put to one side. Using pointed scissors, cut through the soft shell on the belly side.

2 Prise the shell off, leaving the tail attached. (Add to the head; it can be used later for making stock.)

3 Using a small sharp knife, make a shallow cut along the length of the back of the prawn. Use the

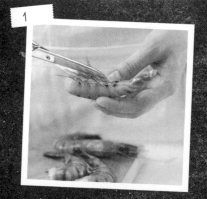

point of the knife to carefully remove and discard the black vein (intestinal tract) that runs along the back of the prawn.

4 To 'butterfly' the prawn, cut halfway through the flesh lengthways from the head end to the base of the tail, and open up the prawn.

4

Langoustines and crayfish

Related to the prawn, langoustines and crayfish can be peeled in the same way as prawns. To extract the meat from langoustine claws, pull off the small pincer from the claws, then work with small scissors to cut open the main section all the way along its length. Split open and carefully pull out the flesh in a single piece. To extract the meat from large crayfish claws, crack them open using a hammer or lobster cracker, then carefully remove the meat.

Also known as scampi, langoustines are at their best when just boiled or steamed, and then eaten from the shells. They can also be used in a shellfish soup.

Crayfish are sold either live or cooked. To cook, boil in court bouillon for 5–10 minutes. Remove from the stock and cool. Eat crayfish from the shell or in a soup.

Prawns and Cucumber in a Spicy Sauce

🍴 **Hands-on time:** 20 minutes, plus standing
Cooking time: about 30 minutes

2 medium cucumbers, halved lengthways, seeded and cut into 2.5cm (1in) chunks
50g (2oz) butter
2 onions, sliced
2 garlic cloves, finely chopped
4 tsp plain flour
2 tsp ground turmeric
1 tsp ground cinnamon
2 tsp sugar
½ tsp ground cloves
750ml (1¼ pints) coconut milk
300ml (½ pint) fish stock
15g (½oz) fresh root ginger, peeled and thinly sliced
3–4 green chillies, thinly sliced (see Safety Tip, page 28)
450g (1lb) raw tiger prawns, peeled and deveined
grated zest and juice of 1 lime
2 tbsp freshly chopped coriander
salt

SAVE TIME

If raw prawns are difficult to find, use cooked ones instead. Add them to the sauce and heat through for 2–3 minutes – no longer or they will become rubbery.

1 Put the cucumber in a colander set over a bowl and sprinkle with salt. Leave for 30 minutes, to allow the salt to extract the excess juices.

2 Melt the butter in a pan, add the onions and garlic and cook for about 5 minutes until softened. Add the flour, turmeric, cinnamon, 1 tsp salt, the sugar and cloves; cook, stirring, for 2 minutes. Add the coconut milk and stock, bring to the boil, reduce the heat and simmer for 5 minutes.

3 Meanwhile, rinse the cucumber thoroughly under cold running water to remove the salt. Add the cucumber, ginger and chillies to the sauce, and cook for a further 10 minutes.

4 Add the prawns to the sauce and cook for a further 5–6 minutes until they turn pink.

5 Just before serving, stir in the lime juice and chopped coriander and sprinkle with lime zest.

Stir-fried Prawns with Cabbage

Hands-on time: 30 minutes
Cooking time: about 7 minutes

2 tbsp vegetable oil

2 garlic cloves, thinly sliced

1 lemongrass stalk, halved and bruised

2 kaffir lime leaves, finely torn

1 small red onion, thinly sliced

1 hot red chilli, seeded and sliced (see
Safety Tip, page 28)

4cm (1½in) piece fresh root ginger,
peeled and cut into long thin shreds

1 tbsp coriander seeds, lightly crushed

450g (1lb) large raw peeled prawns,
deveined

175g (6oz) mangetouts, halved

225g (8oz) pak choi or Chinese
mustard cabbage, torn into
bite-size pieces

2 tbsp Thai fish sauce

juice of 1 lime, or to taste

1 Heat the oil in a wok or large frying pan. Add the garlic, lemongrass, lime leaves, onion, chilli, ginger and coriander seeds and stir-fry for 2 minutes.

2 Add the prawns, mangetouts and pak choi or cabbage, and stir-fry until the vegetables are cooked but still crisp and the prawns are pink and opaque, about 2–3 minutes.

3 Add the fish sauce and lime juice and cook for 1 minute until heated through. Remove the lemongrass and discard; serve immediately.

HEALTHY TIP

Chinese mustard cabbage, otherwise called mustard greens, is a green or red Oriental leaf that has a mild mustard flavour.

Serves 4

Five-minute Stir-fry

Hands-on time: 2 minutes
Cooking time: 5 minutes

1 tbsp sesame oil

175g (6oz) raw peeled tiger prawns, deveined

50ml (2fl oz) ready-made sweet chilli and ginger sauce

225g (8oz) ready-prepared mixed stir-fry vegetables, such as sliced courgettes, broccoli and green beans

1 Heat the oil in a large wok or frying pan, add the prawns and sweet chilli and ginger sauce and stir-fry for 2 minutes.

2 Add the mixed vegetables and stir-fry for a further 2–3 minutes until the prawns are cooked and the vegetables are heated through. Serve immediately.

SAVE EFFORT

For an easy recipe variation, instead of prawns, try chicken cut into strips; stir-fry for 5 minutes in step 1.

Serves 2

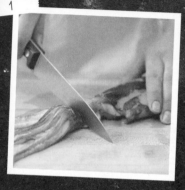

Preparing squid

Sliced into rings or cut into squares, squid is popular in Chinese and South-east Asian cooking.

1 Cut off the tentacles just behind the 'beak'.
2 Pull out the beak and discard. Clean the tentacles well, scraping off as many of the small suckers as you can.
3 Reach inside the body and pull out the internal organs, including the plastic-like 'pen'.

4 Scrape and pull off the loose,
   slippery skin covering the body.
   Rinse the body thoroughly to
   remove all internal organs,
   sand and other debris.
5 Detach the wings and put to one
   side, then cut up the tentacles
   and body as required. To make
   squares, slice the body along
   one side, score diagonally, then
   cut into squares.

4

5

Squid and Vegetables in Black Bean Sauce

🍴 **Hands-on time:** 35 minutes
Cooking time: about 15 minutes

450g (1lb) cleaned squid

2 tbsp sesame seeds

2 tbsp sunflower oil

1 tbsp sesame oil

2 garlic cloves

2 dried red chillies

50g (2oz) broccoli, cut into florets

50g (2oz) mangetouts, trimmed

50g (2oz) carrots, thinly sliced

75g (3oz) cauliflower, cut into
small florets

1 small green or red pepper,
seeded and thinly sliced

50g (2oz) Chinese cabbage or
pak choi, shredded

25g (1oz) bean sprouts

2 tbsp fresh coriander, roughly torn

SAVE EFFORT

Instead of squid, try 400g (14oz)
rump steak, cut into thin strips.

For the sauce:

2 tbsp black bean sauce

1 tbsp Thai fish sauce

2-3 tsp clear honey

75ml (2½fl oz) fish or vegetable stock

1 tbsp tamarind juice

2 tsp cornflour

1 First, prepare the sauce. In a small bowl, mix together the black bean sauce, fish sauce, honey and stock. Add the tamarind juice and cornflour and whisk until smooth. Put to one side.

2 Wash and dry the squid, and halve the tentacles if large. Open out the body pouches, score diagonally, then cut into large squares; put to one side.

3 Toast the sesame seeds in a dry wok or large frying pan over a medium heat, stirring until they turn golden. Tip on to a plate.

4 Heat the sunflower and sesame oil in the same pan. Add the garlic and chillies and fry gently for 5 minutes. Remove the garlic and chillies with a slotted spoon and discard.

5 Add all the vegetables to the pan and stir-fry for 3 minutes. Add the squid, increase the heat and stir-fry for a further 2 minutes until the squid curls up and turns opaque. Add the sauce and allow to simmer for 1 minute.

6 Scatter over the sesame seeds and coriander and serve immediately.

Stir-fried Salmon and Broccoli

Hands-on time: 10 minutes
Cooking time: about 6 minutes

2 tsp sesame oil

1 red pepper, seeded and thinly sliced

½ red chilli, thinly sliced (see Safety
Tip, page 28)

1 garlic clove, crushed

125g (4oz) broccoli florets

2 spring onions, sliced

2 salmon fillets, about 125g (4oz) each,
cut into strips

1 tsp Thai fish sauce

2 tsp soy sauce

wholewheat noodles to serve

1 Heat the oil in a wok or large frying
pan and add the red pepper, chilli,
garlic, broccoli florets and spring
onions. Stir-fry over a high heat for
3–4 minutes.

2 Add the salmon, fish sauce and
soy sauce and cook for 2 minutes,
stirring gently. Serve immediately
with wholewheat noodles.

Serves 2

Perfect Steaming

To use your wok as a steamer you will need a trivet or steamer rack to place inside the wok. The steamer basket (metal or bamboo) sits on the trivet to keep the food above the boiling liquid. Steaming is ideal for fish, chicken and most vegetables.

1. Put the fish or chicken on a lightly oiled heatproof plate that will fit inside the steamer. (Vegetables can be placed directly on the steamer.)
2. Bring the water in the wok or pan to the boil over a medium heat. Put the plate with the fish or chicken in the steamer, cover with a tight-fitting lid and steam until just cooked through (see chart, right).

HEALTHY TIP

Steaming allows food to retain maximum flavour and colour, as well as the vitamins that are easily lost during boiling or poaching.

STEAMING TIMES

Leafy vegetables such as spinach, Chinese leaves	1–2 minutes
Vegetables such as green beans, broccoli, cauliflower, cabbage, carrots	5–8 minutes
Fish fillets	5–10 minutes (allow 10 minutes per 2.5cm (1in) thickness)
Fish steaks and whole fish	15–20 minutes
Chicken	45–50 minutes (depending on whether chicken is shredded, cubed, boned thighs or halved breasts)

Steamed Sesame Salmon

Hands-on time: 20 minutes
Cooking time: about 18 minutes

groundnut or vegetable oil to brush
8–12 large Chinese leaves or
  lettuce leaves
4 salmon steaks, about 150g (5oz) each
½ tsp sesame oil
2 tbsp dry sherry
2 tbsp light soy sauce, plus extra
  to serve
4 spring onions, shredded, plus extra
  spring onion curls to garnish
3 tsp sesame seeds, lightly toasted in
  a dry wok or heavy-based pan
ground white pepper

1 Steam the Chinese leaves or lettuce leaves for 1–2 minutes until soft and pliable. Discard about 2.5cm (1in) of the firm stalk end from each leaf to neaten, and place 2–3 leaves together, slightly overlapping. Put the salmon steaks on top.

2 Mix the sesame oil with the sherry and soy sauce and drizzle the mixture over the salmon. Sprinkle with the shredded spring onions, 2 tsp sesame seeds and ground white pepper to taste.

3 Fold the leaves over the salmon to form neat parcels. Steam for 5–7 minutes or until the fish is cooked and flakes easily.

4 Serve the salmon parcels with the juices spooned over. Sprinkle with the remaining sesame seeds and a little extra soy sauce, then garnish with spring onion curls.

SAVE EFFORT

To make perfect spring onion curls, trim spring onions into 7.5cm (3in) lengths, shred finely, then place in a bowl of water with ice cubes for 30 minutes.

Serves 4

Teriyaki Salmon with Spinach

Hands-on time: 10 minutes, plus marinating
Cooking time: 6 minutes

550g (1¼lb) salmon fillet,
 cut into 1cm (½in) slices
3 tbsp teriyaki sauce
3 tbsp tamari or light soy sauce
2 tbsp vegetable oil
1 tbsp sesame oil
1 tbsp chopped fresh chives
2 tsp grated fresh root ginger
2 garlic cloves, crushed
350g (12oz) soba noodles
350g (12oz) baby spinach leaves
furikake seasoning

1 Gently mix the salmon slices with the teriyaki sauce, then cover, chill and leave to marinate for 1 hour.
2 Mix together the tamari or light soy sauce, 1 tbsp vegetable oil, sesame oil, chives, ginger and garlic. Put to one side.
3 Cook the noodles according to the pack instructions. Drain and put to one side.
4 Heat the remaining vegetable oil in a wok or large frying pan. Remove the salmon from the marinade and add it to the pan. Cook over a high heat until it turns opaque – about 30 seconds. Remove from the pan and put to one side.
5 Add the drained noodles to the pan and stir until warmed through. Stir in the spinach and cook for 1-2 minutes until wilted. Add the soy sauce mixture and stir to combine.

HEALTHY TIPS

Furikake seasoning is a Japanese condiment consisting of sesame seeds and chopped seaweed which can be found in major supermarkets and Asian food shops.
Soba noodles are made from buckwheat and are gluten-free. If you have a wheat allergy or gluten intolerance, look for 100% soba on the pack.

Serves 4

6 Divide the noodles among four deep
bowls, then top with the salmon.
Sprinkle with furikake seasoning
and serve.

Hearty Dishes

Stir-frying Poultry and Meat

Stir-frying is a healthy and speedy way to cook poultry and other tender cuts of meat.

Preparing and cooking

1 Trim off any fat, then cut the poultry or meat into even-size strips or dice no more than 5mm (¼in) thick. Heat a wok or large pan until hot and add oil to coat the inside.

2 Add the poultry or meat and cook, stirring constantly, until just done. Remove and put to one side. Cook the other ingredients you are using for the stir-fry, then put the poultry or meat back into the pan and cook for 1–2 minutes to heat through.

HEALTHY TIP

Stir-frying in a wok uses less fat than other frying techniques, and cooking briefly over a high heat retains as many nutrients as possible.

Slicing breast fillets

1 Cut or pull out the long strip of flesh lying on the inside of the breast. Slice it across the grain to the thickness required for your recipe. (Raw chicken should not be cut less than about 3mm/⅛in thick.)

2 Starting at the small tip of the breast, cut slices of the required thickness. Alternatively, cut into chunks or dice.

Perfect slicing

To make slicing easier, put breast fillets in the freezer for 30 minutes or so before slicing. The flesh will be much firmer and it will therefore be easier to slice it thinly.

2

Pork Stir-fry with Chilli and Mango

Hands-on time: 5 minutes
Cooking time: about 10 minutes

75g (3oz) medium egg noodles

1 tsp groundnut oil

½ red chilli, seeded and finely chopped (see Safety Tip, page 28)

125g (4oz) pork stir-fry strips

1 head pak choi, roughly chopped

1 tbsp soy sauce

½ ripe mango, sliced

1 Bring a large pan of water to the boil and cook the noodles for about 4 minutes or according to the pack instructions. Drain, then plunge into cold water. Put to one side.

2 Meanwhile, heat the oil in a wok or large frying pan until very hot. Add the chilli and pork and stir-fry for 3–4 minutes. Add the pak choi and soy sauce and cook for a further 2–3 minutes. Add the mango and toss to combine.

3 Drain the noodles and add them to the pan. Toss well and cook for 1–2 minutes until heated through. Serve immediately.

Serves 4

Sweet and Sour Pork Stir-fry

Hands-on time: 15 minutes
Cooking time: about 10 minutes

2 tbsp vegetable oil

350g (12oz) pork fillet, cut into finger-size pieces

1 red onion, finely sliced

1 red pepper, seeded and finely sliced

2 carrots, cut into thin strips

3 tbsp sweet chilli sauce

1 tbsp white wine vinegar

220g can pineapple slices, chopped, with 2 tbsp juice put to one side

a large handful of bean sprouts

½ tbsp sesame seeds

a large handful of fresh coriander, roughly chopped

salt and freshly ground black pepper

boiled long-grain rice to serve

1 Heat the oil over a high heat in a large frying pan or wok. Add the pork, onion, red pepper and carrots and cook for 3–5 minutes, stirring frequently, until the meat is cooked through and the vegetables are softening.

2 Stir in the chilli sauce, vinegar and reserved pineapple juice and bring to the boil, then stir in the pineapple chunks and bean sprouts and heat through.

3 Check the seasoning. Scatter the sesame seeds and coriander over and serve immediately with rice.

SAVE TIME

As with all stir-fries, have everything sliced and ready before you start cooking.

Serves 4

Turkey and Sesame Stir-fry with Noodles

Hands-on time: 5 minutes, plus 5 minutes marinating
Cooking time: 10 minutes

300g (11oz) turkey breast fillets, cut into thin strips

3 tbsp teriyaki marinade

3 tbsp clear honey

500g (1lb 2oz) medium egg noodles

about 1 tbsp sesame oil, plus extra for the noodles

300g (11oz) ready-prepared mixed stir-fry vegetables, such as carrots, broccoli, red cabbage, mangetouts, bean sprouts and purple spring onions

2 tbsp sesame seeds, lightly toasted in a dry wok or heavy-based pan

1 Put the turkey strips in a large bowl with the teriyaki marinade and honey, and stir to coat. Cover and set aside for 5 minutes.

2 Bring a large pan of water to the boil and cook the noodles for about 4 minutes or according to the packet instructions. Drain well, then toss in a little sesame oil.

3 Heat 1 tbsp of the oil in a wok or large frying pan and add the turkey, reserving the marinade. Stir-fry over a very high heat for 2–3 minutes until cooked through and beginning to brown. Add a drop more oil, if needed, then add the vegetables and reserved marinade. Continue to cook over a high heat, stirring, until the vegetables have started to soften and the sauce is warmed through.

4 Scatter with the sesame seeds and serve immediately with the noodles.

Serves 4

Orange and Ginger Beef Stir-fry

🍴 **Hands-on time:** 15 minutes
Cooking time: about 8 minutes

1 tbsp cornflour
75ml (3fl oz) smooth orange juice
2 tbsp soy sauce
1 tbsp vegetable oil
400g (14oz) beef stir-fry strips
5cm (2in) piece fresh root ginger, peeled and cut into matchsticks
300g pack mixed stir-fry vegetables of your choice, chopped if large
1 tbsp sesame seeds
salt and freshly ground black pepper
egg noodles to serve

1 Put the cornflour into a small bowl and gradually whisk in the orange juice followed by the soy sauce to make a smooth mixture. Put to one side.

2 Heat the oil over a high heat in a large frying pan or wok. Add the beef strips and stir-fry for 1–2 minutes. Stir in the ginger, vegetables and a splash of water and stir-fry until the vegetables are just tender and the beef is cooked to your liking.

3 Add the orange juice mixture to the pan and cook, stirring occasionally, until thick and syrupy – about 30 seconds. Check the seasoning and sprinkle the sesame seeds over. Serve immediately with egg noodles.

Serves 4

Szechuan Beef

Hands-on time: 15 minutes, plus marinating
Cooking time: about 10 minutes

350g (12oz) beef skirt or rump steak, cut into thin strips

5 tbsp hoisin sauce

4 tbsp dry sherry

2 tbsp vegetable oil

2 red or green chillies, finely chopped (see Safety Tip, page 28)

1 large onion, thinly sliced

2 garlic cloves, crushed

2 red peppers, seeded and cut into diamond shapes

2.5cm (1in) piece fresh root ginger, peeled and grated

225g can bamboo shoots, drained and sliced

1 tbsp sesame oil

1 Put the beef in a bowl, add the hoisin sauce and sherry and stir to coat. Cover and leave to marinate for 30 minutes.

2 Heat the vegetable oil in a wok or large frying pan until smoking hot. Add the chillies, onion and garlic and stir-fry over a medium heat for 3–4 minutes until softened. Remove with a slotted spoon and put to one side. Add the red peppers, increase the heat and stir-fry for a few seconds. Remove from the pan and put to one side.

3 Add the steak and marinade to the pan in batches. Stir-fry each batch over a high heat for about 1 minute, removing with a slotted spoon.

4 Put the vegetables back into the pan. Add the ginger and bamboo shoots, then the beef, and stir-fry for a further 1 minute until heated through. Transfer to a warmed serving dish, sprinkle the sesame oil over the top and serve immediately.

Teriyaki Beef Stir-fry

Hands-on time: 20 minutes, plus marinating
Cooking time: about 8 minutes

450g (1lb) beef fillet, sliced as
   thinly as possible, then cut into
   1cm (½in) wide strips
2 tbsp vegetable or groundnut oil
225g (8oz) carrots, cut into matchsticks
½ cucumber, seeded and cut into
   matchsticks
4–6 spring onions, thinly sliced
   diagonally
noodles tossed in a little sesame oil
   and wasabi paste (optional) to serve

For the teriyaki marinade:

4 tbsp tamari
4 tbsp mirin or medium sherry
1 garlic clove, finely chopped
2.5cm (1in) piece fresh root ginger,
   peeled and finely chopped

1 First, make the marinade. Put all
the ingredients for the marinade
in a shallow bowl and mix well. Add
the beef and turn to coat. Cover and
marinate in the fridge for at least
30 minutes, preferably overnight.

2 Drain the beef, keeping any
marinade to one side. Heat a wok
or large frying pan, then add the oil
and heat until it is smoking. Add
the carrots, cucumber and spring
onions and fry over a high heat for
2 minutes until the edges are well
browned. Remove from the pan and
put to one side.

3 Add the beef to the pan and stir-fry
over a very high heat for 2 minutes.

4 Put the vegetables back into the
pan and add the reserved marinade.
Stir-fry for 1–2 minutes until heated
through. Serve with noodles tossed
in a little sesame oil and a small
amount of wasabi paste if you like.

Serves 4

Quick Turkey and Pork Stir-fry

Hands-on time: 15 minutes
Cooking time: about 10 minutes

1 tbsp vegetable oil

200g (7oz) turkey breast, cut into
finger-size strips

200g (7oz) pork loin fillet, cut into
finger-size strips

1 tbsp Chinese 5-spice powder

1 each yellow and orange pepper,
seeded and sliced

150g (5oz) pak choi, thickly shredded

1 tsp sesame seeds

1–1½ tbsp soy sauce, to taste

a large handful of fresh coriander

salt and freshly ground black pepper

1 Heat the oil in a large wok or frying pan over a high heat and add the turkey and pork. Cook for 3 minutes, stirring occasionally. Add the Chinese 5-spice powder, the sliced peppers, pak choi and a splash of water.

2 Continue to cook for a few minutes until the vegetables are just tender (but retaining a crunch) and the meat is cooked through (add more water as needed).

3 Sprinkle over the sesame seeds, add the soy sauce and rip in the coriander. Check the seasoning and serve with noodles or rice if you like.

SAVE EFFORT

If you prefer not to mix the two meats, then simply make up the volume using one or the other.

Serves 4

Chicken with Peanut Sauce

Hands-on time: 10 minutes, plus marinating
Cooking time: about 10 minutes

4 skinless chicken breast fillets,
   cut into strips
1 tbsp ground coriander
2 garlic cloves, finely chopped
4 tbsp vegetable oil
2 tbsp clear honey
Thai fragrant rice to serve
fresh coriander sprigs to garnish

For the peanut sauce:
1 tbsp vegetable oil
2 tbsp curry paste
2 tbsp brown sugar
2 tbsp peanut butter
200ml (7fl oz) coconut milk

1 Mix the chicken with the ground coriander, garlic, oil and honey. Cover, chill and leave to marinate for 15 minutes.

2 To make the peanut sauce, heat the oil in a pan, add the curry paste, brown sugar and peanut butter and fry for 1 minute. Add the coconut milk and bring to the boil, stirring all the time, then reduce the heat and simmer for 5 minutes.

3 Meanwhile, heat a wok or large frying pan and, when hot, stir-fry the chicken and its marinade in batches for 3–4 minutes or until cooked, adding more oil if needed.

4 Serve the chicken on a bed of Thai fragrant rice, with the peanut sauce poured over. Garnish with coriander sprigs.

SAVE EFFORT

For an easy alternative, replace the chicken with pork escalopes or rump steak, cut into thin strips.

Serves 4

Sesame Lamb

Hands-on time: 15 minutes
Cooking time: 15 minutes

125g (4oz) fresh white breadcrumbs
50g (2oz) sesame seeds
450g (1lb) lean boneless lamb, cut into 5mm (¼in) thick slices
2 medium eggs, beaten
6 tbsp groundnut or sunflower oil
1 onion, sliced
3 carrots, cut into strips
225g (8oz) broccoli, cut into florets
2.5cm (1in) piece fresh root ginger, peeled and grated
450ml (¾ pint) chicken stock
2 tbsp dry sherry
1½ tbsp cornflour
1 tbsp dark soy sauce
salt and freshly ground black pepper
a few drops of sesame oil to serve

1 Mix the breadcrumbs with the sesame seeds and season with salt and ground black pepper. Dip the lamb slices in the beaten egg, then coat them in the breadcrumb mixture, pressing the breadcrumbs on firmly with your fingertips.

2 Heat 2 tbsp oil in a wok or large frying pan, add half the lamb slices and fry for about 2 minutes on each side until golden. Remove from the pan, drain and keep warm. Cook the remaining lamb in the same way, using another 2 tbsp oil.

3 Wipe the pan clean and heat the remaining oil. Add the onion, carrots, broccoli and ginger and stir-fry for 2 minutes. Add the stock and sherry, cover and cook the vegetables for 1 minute.

4 Blend the cornflour and soy sauce with 1 tbsp water. Stir the mixture into the pan and cook for 2 minutes, stirring constantly. Put the lamb slices back into the pan and cook for 1–2 minutes until heated through. Sprinkle with sesame oil and serve.

SAVE EFFORT

For an easy alternative, try this with slices of turkey breast.

Serves 4

Calorie Gallery

30 cal ♥ 1g protein
1.5g fat (trace sat)
2g fibre ♥ 3g carb ♥ 0g salt

10

75 cal ♥ 2g protein
6g fat (1g sat) ♥ 1g fibre
2g carb ♥ 0.1g salt

12

110 cal ♥ 2g protein
3g fat (trace sat) ♥ 0.8g fibre
19g carb ♥ 0.8g salt

14

224 cal ♥ 2g protein
13g fat (2g sat) ♥ 2g fibre
23g carb ♥ 0.7g salt

20

338 cal ♥ 37g protein
10g fat (3g sat) ♥ 2g fibre
27g carb ♥ 1.7g salt

34

215 cal ♥ 15g protein
13g fat (3g sat) ♥ 1g fibre
11g carb ♥ 1.2g salt

36

515 cal ♥ 40g protein
35g fat (25g sat) ♥ 1g fibre
9g carb ♥ 0.8g salt

40

318 cal ♥ 20g protein
20g fat (12g sat) ♥ 3g fibre
14g carb ♥ 0.3g salt

52

160 cal ♥ 26g protein
5g fat (1g sat) ♥ 2g fibre
5g carb ♥ 1.1g salt

54

397 cal ♥ 25g protein
25g fat (8g sat) ♥ 2g fibre
17g carb ♥ 0.4g salt

56

412 cal ♥ 21g protein
18g fat (3g sat) ♥ 2g fibre
46g carb ♥ 1.9g salt

72

403 cal ♥ 25g protein
10g fat (2g sat) ♥ 4g fibre
62g carb ♥ 0.7g salt

74

431 cal ♥ 12g protein
15g fat (3g sat) ♥ 2g fibre
61g carb ♥ 2.1g salt

78

451 cal ♥ 27g protein
13g fat (3g sat) ♥ 2g fibre
56g carb ♥ 2.6g salt

80

450 cal ♥ 7g protein
21g fat (3g sat) ♥ 5g fibre
55g carb ♥ 2.1g salt

568 cal ♥ 11g protein
29g fat (4g sat) ♥ 6g fibre
65g carb ♥ 2.9g salt

334 cal ♥ 28g protein
11g fat ♥ 1g fibre
32g carb ♥ 4.0g salt

26

28

266 cal ♥ 12g protein
11g fat (2g sat) ♥ 0.6g fibre
33g carb ♥ 0.8g salt

30

252 cal ♥ 31g protein
8g fat (1g sat) ♥ 0.7g fibre
9g carb ♥ 2.2g salt

118 cal ♥ 28g protein
3g fat (0.5g sat) ♥ 4g fibre
13g carb ♥ 1.3g salt

253 cal ♥ 31g protein
13g fat (9g sat) ♥ 0.4g fibre
2g carb ♥ 2.5g salt

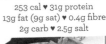

247 cal ♥ 22g protein
16g fat (11g sat) ♥ 0.1g fibre
4g carb ♥ 0.8g salt

44

46

48

660 cal ♥ 37g protein
31g fat (11g sat) ♥ 3g fibre
57g carb ♥ 1.6g salt

157 cal ♥ 4g protein
5g fat (1g sat) ♥ 1g fibre
22g carb ♥ 0.5g salt

595 cal ♥ 30g protein
45g fat (24g sat) ♥ 2g fibre
18g carb ♥ 1.2g salt

339 cal ♥ 25g protein
11g fat (2g sat) ♥ 3g fibre
37g carb ♥ 0.4g salt

3

60

66

70

476 cal ♥ 34g protein
8g fat (2g sat) ♥ 5g fibre
64g carb ♥ 3.4g salt

451 cal ♥ 35g protein
11g fat (2g sat) ♥ 4g fibre
59g carb ♥ 1.3g salt

335 cal ♥ 28g protein
4g fat (1g sat) ♥ 3g fibre
46g carb ♥ 1.0g salt

408 cal ♥ 18g protein
20g fat (5g sat) ♥ 2g fibre
38g carb ♥ 1.2g salt

84

86

88

306 cal ♥ 23g protein
11g fat (3g sat) ♥ 0.3g fibre
31g carb ♥ 2g salt

90

113 cal ♥ 3g protein
9g fat (1g sat) ♥ 3g fibre
6g carb ♥ 0.1g salt

94

167 cal ♥ 9g protein
11g fat (2g sat) ♥ 4g fibre
5g carb ♥ 1.6g salt

98

157cal ♥ 8g protein
9g fat (1g sat) ♥ 3g fibre
11g carb ♥ 1.1g salt

100

334 cal ♥ 13g protein
11g fat (2g sat) ♥ 3g fibre
49g carb ♥ 1.5g salt

112

317 cal ♥ 2g protein
14g fat (2g sat) ♥ 0.6g fibre
43g carb ♥ 1.7g salt

114

334 cal ♥ 18g protein
8g fat (2g sat) ♥ 2g fibre
51g carb ♥ 3.5g salt

118

170 cal ♥ 21g protein
7g fat (1g sat) ♥ 3g fibre
11g carb ♥ 1.6g salt

134

274 cal ♥ 20g protein
15g fat (2g sat) ♥ 2g fibre
12g carb ♥ 1g salt

138

279 cal ♥ 29g protein
15g fat (3g sat) ♥ 3g fibre
7g carb ♥ 0.4g salt

140

672 cal ♥ 43g protein
18g fat (4.2g sat) ♥ 6g fibre
97g carb ♥ 0.7g salt

156

220 cal ♥ 23g protein
10g fat (3g sat) ♥ 2g fibre
8g carb ♥ 0.7g salt

158

298 cal ♥ 26g protein
14g fat (4g sat) ♥ 3g fibre
15g carb ♥ 0.6g salt

160

275 cal ♥ 24g protein
16g fat (5g sat) ♥ 2g fibre
6g carb ♥ 2g salt

162

445 cal ♥ 11g protein
?g fat (9g sat) ♥ 3g fibre
60g carb ♥ 2g salt

2

136 cal ♥ 2g protein
7g fat (1g sat) ♥ 3g fibre
17g carb ♥ 2.5g salt

104

149 cal ♥ 4g protein
9g fat (1g sat) ♥ 3g fibre
14g carb ♥ 0.7g salt

108

232 cal ♥ 14g protein
18g fat (4g sat) ♥ 3g fibre
6g carb ♥ 0.9g salt

110

197 cal ♥ 30g protein
7g fat (1g sat) ♥ 1g fibre
6g carb ♥ 2g salt

2

335 cal ♥ 19g protein
25g fat (17g sat) ♥ 0.2g fibre
8g carb ♥ 1.6g salt

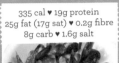

126

580 cal ♥ 24g protein
47g fat (24g sat) ♥ 2g fibre
27g carb ♥ 2.5g salt

130

193 cal ♥ 22g protein
8g fat (1g sat) ♥ 2g fibre
7g carb ♥ 1.4g salt

132

312 cal ♥ 31g protein
19g fat (3g sat) ♥ 0.7g fibre
2g carb ♥ 1.5g salt

672 cal ♥ 40g protein
30g fat (4g sat) ♥ 4g fibre
66g carb ♥ 2.9g salt

4

146

302 cal ♥ 21g protein
9g fat (3g sat) ♥ 4g fibre
36g carb ♥ 0.4g salt

152

281 cal ♥ 21g protein
15g fat (3g sat) ♥ 3g fibre
16g carb ♥ 1.9g salt

154

210 cal ♥ 30g protein
8g fat (2g sat) ♥ 2g fibre
5g carb ♥ 0.9g salt

661 cal ♥ 35g protein
41g fat (10g sat) ♥ 5g fibre
40g carb ♥ 2.3g salt

510 cal ♥ 41g protein
34g fat (12g sat) ♥ 0.5g fibre
9g carb ♥ 0.5g salt

4

166

168

Index

PICTURE CREDITS
Photographers:
Steve Baxter (page 155);
Martin Brigdale (pages 11, 13, 1, 25,
41, 43, 49, 53, 55, 57, 59, 61, 67, 68,
69, 71, 73, 75, 79, 81, 83, 85, 87, 89,
91, 95, 99, 101, 103, 105, 109, 111, 113,
115, 119, 123, 127, 131, 135, 139, 141,
145, 147, 157, 161, 163, 167 and 169);
Nicki Dowey (pages 27, 31 and 47);
Gareth Morgans (pages 15, 35,
119, 159 and 165); Craig Robertson
(pages 9, 18T, 22, 37, 38, 64, 75, 106,
107, 120, 121, 124, 125, 128,
129, 136, 137, 142, 150 and 151);
Lucinda Symons (pages 16, 18B
and 153); Jon Whitaker (pages 29
and 45).

Home Economists:
Anna Bujrges-Lumsden,
Joanna Farrow, Emma Jane Frost,
Teresa Goldfinch, Alice Hart,
Lucy McKelvie, Kim Morphew,
Aya Nishimura, Katie Rogers,
Bridget Sargeson, Stella Sargeson,
Jennifer White and Mari Mererid
Wiliams.

Stylists:
Tamzin Ferdinando, Wei Tang,
Helen Trent and Fanny Ward.

BAKE ME A CAKE
There's always time for cake

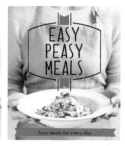

EASY PEASY MEALS
Easy meals for every day

LET'S DO BRUNCH
Mouth-watering meals to start your day

CHEAP EATS
Budget-busting ideas that won't break the bank

SALAD DAYS
Oh-so-fresh ideas for fabulous salads

Available online at store.anovabooks.com and from all good bookshops

POSH NOSH
Delicious recipes to impress your guests

PARTY FOOD
Delicious recipes to get the party started

SLOW STOPPERS
Slow-cooked meals packed with flavour

GREAT VEG
Inspired ideas for delicious veggie meals

AL FRESCO EATS
Easy grills, barbecues and picnics

ROAST IT
There's nothing better than a delicious roast

FLASH IN THE PAN
Spice up your noodles and stir-fries

GLUTEN-FREE AND EASY
Oh-so-good-for-you recipes that taste great

LOW FAT LOW CAL
Nice recipes don't need to be naughty